Grandma Was a Sailmaker

Tales of the Cajun Wetlands

by
Verne Pitre

Illustrated by
Billy Ledet

Blue Heron Press

Thibodaux, Louisiana

Grandma Was a Sailmaker

Copyright © 1991 by Verne Pitre
All rights reserved.
Illustrations Copyright © 1991 Blue Heron Press
All rights reserved.
Manufactured in the United States of America

Blue Heron Press
100 W. 5th St.
Thibodaux, LA 70301
(504) 446-8201

ISBN 0-9621724-5-6
Library of Congress Catalog Card Number 91 - 90466

DEDICATION

This excursion backward in time is dedicated to my wife, Ouida, who was the first to critique the essays; to my children Jackie, Dennis, and Darlene; to all my grandchildren, whom you will meet in the essay entitled, The Good Old Days, but especially to granddaughter Ryan Kathleen Mire.

From her earliest years, Ryan's proximity and her abundant love for stories generated hours and hours of sharing with her overjoyed grandparents. Her oft' repeated request, "Tell me about when you were little," always was a reminder of yet another adventure or misadventure to be recalled, recounted, and enjoyed. Added to the uncounted volumes of stories read aloud together, these were experiences which shall be remembered forever.

Grandma Was a Sailmaker

FOREWARD

Collectively, the essays contained herein are the thoughts and beliefs of a Cajun grandfather who is proud of his heritage. Individually, the essays are return trips into a boyhood of the 1920's and 30's, with a few relating to the 1940's.

During most of my adult life I facetiously have referred to my childhood as a period of "growing up fat, dumb, and happy." In reflection upon these essays, I am convinced only of the correctness of the first two parts of this observation. I was chubby and I was naive. I thought I was happy. But while writing these essays, I have been genuinely surprised, maybe shocked, to realize that the most vivid of my childhood memories are tinged with some form of sadness, however amusing these may seem today.

Perhaps it was growing up as a "depression era kid" which caused this. Perhaps it was my personality. I have always been more of a loner than gregarious. Or, maybe one tends to recall easiest the more painful episodes of life -- the misadventures, so to speak. Whatever, I blame neither my parents, who were good, moral, hardworking folks, nor anyone else who may have helped to form me into what I am today.

People names have been left out of some essays. This was done neither to protect nor to slight. There knowingly is included nothing which I believe to be demeaning or less than factual. Rather, such decisions were made when inclusions would not have added significantly to the story. The contributions of all who influenced the substance of even one essay, either by circumstance or by design, are cheerfully acknowledged, although these contributors may be

Grandma Was a Sailmaker

known only to themselves and me.

I especially thank two of my cousins, Enosia Gaspard Savoie and Lawrence Gaspard, as well as Warren Authement for helping me recall data which would have remained vague in my memory. Lastly, I am grateful to my friend Billy Ledet, who did the illustrations, and to my publisher, Carolyn Portier Gorman, for being such a joy to work with.

– Verne Pitre

CONTENTS

Grandma Was a Sailmaker

A FORK FULL

The bayou country of southcentral Louisiana is an incredibly interesting and startling environment. It consists mainly of large, marshy areas with numerous inhabited ridges punctuated by moss-covered oak and cypress trees centuries old. Before reaching Lafourche Parish, Bayou Lafourche flows from the Mississippi River at Donaldsonville, through the parishes of Ascension and Assumption. It runs the length of the parish before emptying into the Gulf of Mexico. The bayou began unknown centuries ago when the Mississippi altered its course southeastward, creating a two-prong fork (la fourche).

Early map-makers named the old river bed "La Fourche des Chitimachas" (the fork of the Chitimachas) after an Indian tribe inhabiting the area. Later, the name was shortened to "La Fourche" and finally the spelling changed to the single word, "Lafourche".

French, Spanish, English, and German settlements appeared along the banks of Bayou Lafourche in the early 1700's. The first Acadians did not arrive until several years following their imprisonment and exile from Nova Scotia by the British beginning in 1755. Cajuns now live mainly in the civil parishes (elsewhere counties) of southwest and southcentral Louisiana. At first, we were known as Acadians. Today, we are more often called Cajuns. We answer proudly to either.

Grandma Was a Sailmaker

There are recognized currently two groups of Cajuns. Ancestors of the Prairie Cajuns settled the open prairies of southwest Louisiana and developed a lifestyle largely associated with cattle raising and growing rice, vegetables, and sugar cane crops.

The Wetlands or Bayou Cajuns settled the bayous of southcentral Louisiana and devoted themselves to hunting, trapping, and fishing, as well as to rice, cotton, and sugar cane farming. The site of Nicholls State University in Thibodaux was once a rice, then sugar cane farm. By the 1940's, cotton had almost completely given way to sugar cane in Lafourche Parish and rice as a crop had disappeared entirely.

Louisiana became a state in 1803. Lafourche Parish was created in 1805 when the Territory of Orleans was divided into 12 parishes. Before Lafourche became thickly populated all settlers lived along its bayou banks. Most land grants were narrow in width and very deep, usually extending 40 arpents from the bank. (An arpent is 192 linear feet, approximately five-sixths of an acre.)

Most farms, therefore, had a rather narrow frontage on the bayou with the long dimension extending perpendicular inward for 7,680 feet. The strips grew more and more narrow as aging fathers divided their property with their children. Each child was given a part of the higher and more fertile bayou-side ridge extending into the less desirable marshy bottom land (often marsh-land) and culminating at the 40 arpent line.

The bayou continued to distribute water from the Mississippi. Spring flooding, though beneficially enriching farmlands with sediment, was a severe problem. Strictly enforced laws held each landowner responsible for building and maintaining a bayou-side levee across the front of his property and for connecting this with the corresponding levee of each neighbor, thereby creating a single levee on each side of the bayou. The levees became obsolete when Bayou Lafourche was dammed at the Mississippi in 1903. Fresh water flow into the bayou is maintained today by a pumping station located atop the dam in Donaldsonville.

The northern portion of Lafourche Parish is mainly agricultural. Sugar cane farming is the chief activity, with some truck farming occurring. Further south, commercial fishing and oil field industries dominate. Shrimping is the largest of the fishing activities of Lafourche Parish, but oyster cultivation and harvesting play an important part in the economy.

Although relatively new, crawfish ponds dot the length of the parish and constitute a growing source of revenue. Trapping has declined but still furnishes a significant portion of the furs which keep Louisiana first among fur-producing states.

Fourchon, at the mouth of Bayou Lafourche, is the site of America's first superport. It bustles with oil-related activity while it provides a safe harbor for supply boats, shrimp luggers, and pleasure craft. Offshore, mooring buoys enable huge tankers to unload foreign oil into a gigantic pipeline leading to storage and refining facilities miles away.

Cajun cuisine is world renown and restaurants of note can be found throughout Lafourche Parish. Patrons can enjoy a wide variety of well-seasoned fish, shrimp, oyster, crawfish and crab delicacies year round.

Lafourche is a fork veritably full of history, natural resources, products, and serious but fun-loving people. It is a bit of Cajun geography which lives up to the ancestral motto, *Laissez Les Bon Temps Rouler* (Let The Good Times Roll), but examplifies that industriousness is what allows the good times.

Grandma Was a Sailmaker

Grandma
Was a
Sailmaker

Tales of the Cajun Wetlands

~1~

GRANDMA
WAS A SAILMAKER

Tall ships graced the large harbor. Some navigated amid an endless variety of other craft. Others lay at anchor, silently keeping alive the memory of America's youth.

Mostly, these were replicas of the exploratory caravels of the fifteenth though eighteenth centuries or of the fast, slender, American clipper ships developed during the early nineteenth century, aboard which had been carried out the daring exploits of strong men in a man's world. Today, however, it was the memory of a strong woman in a man's world which returned to my attention.

My part-Acadian maternal grandmother, Marie Annelie Bruce Gaspard (known to everyone as "Tante Nel"), toiled alongside her husband to produce sails, tents, and tarpaulins for smaller ships critical to domestic transportation, commerce, and the seafood industry of south Louisiana. Dwarfed by the tall ships, these sailing vessels plied the bayous, rivers, and the Gulf of Mexico.

I recall being told that Grandma and Grandpa outfitted a great portion of these. "Your grandpa and I worked almost every day making sails during the five years after our marriage in 1901," Grandma said.

1

Grandma Was a Sailmaker

Grandma was a person you really could have liked if you like exceptional grandmothers. I knew her always as white-headed, matronly, stout, hard-working, interesting, caring, and kind. She walked first with one cane, then two, but she didn't let her ailments take control. I never knew Grandpa. He died where they lived in the community of Cote Blanche in Lafourche Parish in 1906, a victim of Bright's Disease. I was born 20 years later. But Grandma and his son from a first marriage were responsible for my strong feeling that I did know him.

Grandpa was chief of the sailmaking operation. He had expertise gleaned from years spent in and among boats. Grandma managed to keep busy caring for his children from his earlier marriage and their daughter, my mother. Then, of course, there was cooking, canning fruits and vegetables, grinding coffee beans, making yeast cakes, kneading dough and baking bread in the outdoor clay oven, drawing gallons of water from the outdoor cistern for washing and drinking, feeding the chickens, gathering eggs, and sewing.

Fortunately for Grandma, there was not the luxury of a cow to milk, cream to separate, or butter to churn. Otherwise, she might never have found time to become proficient in sailmaking. She did, though, and she worked side-by-side with Grandpa, laying out the patterns for sails on the ground, then cutting and sewing. Typically, the sails they made were square at the bottom or foot, with sloping top or head and one sloping side—the leech or luft. They laid out each pattern by driving pegs into the ground and attaching string between these to form the perimeter.

Strips of heavy, white canvas cloth were cut and placed side by side and upright (for greater strength) within the pattern. A generous overlap was allowed at each seam. When the sail had been formed, sewing began.

Heavy twine, coated with beeswax for water-proofing, prevention of raveling, and avoidance of tangles, was threaded through the eye of a long, large needle. The seams were then hand-sewn together. A pommel, thimble-like leather and metal device worn around the palm of the hand, forced the needle through the heavy canvas, propelled by a push of the palm. Later, when demand for their sails became too great for hand-sewing, Grandpa and Grandma sought speed on Grandma's pedal-powered sewing machine. But much handwork remained.

The sails they made contained many eyelets on the perimeter for attaching ropes. This permitted canvas to be let out or taken in, as wind velocity dictated. In strong winds, a minimum of sail would be put up while on much calmer days the canvas was pulled completely to the top of the mast.

"Grandpa never liked metal eyelets," Grandma said, "because they tore out of the canvas too easily. We made rope eyelets out of twisted strands of strong fiber." These were pounded into the right size on a round iron tool with one tapered end. The finished eyelets were then hand-sewn around holes pre-cut in the sail's hem.

I never had the privilege of seeing a sail bearing the stenciling, "M. Gaspard, Sailmaker, Lafourche, La.", which was how Grandpa identified their handi-work. His pommel and a hand sewing needle are now part of the permanent collection at the Center for Traditional Boat Building, Nicholls State University, in Thibodaux, Louisiana.

The copper stencil did not fare as well. When I was in high school, I discovered it in the old corn crib behind the house. But I was not knowledgeable enough then about the worth of artifacts to take the necessary steps for its preservation. Consequently, it has become lost. A newspaper photograph of the stencil does exist -- part of a 1942 newspaper feature article about World War II engine shortages forcing a possible return to the use of sails.

Tall ships carried crewmen skilled in sailmaking and sail repairs. Not so the small, domestic sail craft. These depended upon land people like Grandma. Grandma died in 1955 at the age of 88. But not before she had developed far greater skills than expected of the typical housewife and mother of her day. She left a significant mark in what was then a man's world, served as a rich source of family lore, and enriched my life immeasurably with kind and gentle experiences which I will cherish forever.

~2~

HOME AWAY FROM HOME

When I was very young, my father (known to everyone as I. J.) earned the living for our family by trapping for pelts in winter and trawling for shrimp the rest of the year. While trawling, he was away for days—sometimes a week or two if the catch was unusually good. I missed his presence and, looking back, feel that we may have lost out on father-son relationships possible only when the father is home every night.

Winters were more enjoyable because Mother and I were able to accompany Daddy to the trapping grounds for the full four-month season. Our home while away from home was a houseboat pulled to the site by a shrimp lugger in time for the November opening. Daddy's boat did the pulling and was named "Rhode Island". How or why that came to be its name, I do not know. I do remember feeling that it was such a glorious name— much better than those of boats reporting the names of people.

Our houseboat was neither palatial nor luxurious, as such boats now tend to be. It was a rectangular wooden barge, about 12 X 28 feet, with a four-foot porch across each end. It was moored alongside the bayou bank and tied to pilings driven into the water. Access to land was by means of a 6 X 12 inch board or "gang plank" reaching from "rear" porch to the bank.

The outside was unpainted wood siding topped by a flat roof covered with tar paper. The inside was divided crossways into two 12 X 10 rooms with a doorway between. Both had a single window on each side wall and a door in the end wall leading to its own porch. One of the rooms was for meal preparation and eating, the other for sleeping.

A small pot-bellied stove used continually for heating or cooking bellowed smoke by way of a tin pipe extending through the roof. It was accompanied by a small table and three or four armless chairs. Provisions (staple groceries) were mostly kept in stacked boxes in one corner, but rice, sugar, and flour remained in sacks. Meat, with the exception of a salt pork shoulder kept inaccessible to four-legged and two-legged varmints by being hung on the "front" porch (no gang plank there), was provided fresh through Daddy's frequent early morning hunts.

In the sleeping room there was a double bed for Mother and Daddy and a small wallside bunk for me. Clothing was stored somewhere in the room, but I remember neither furniture nor containers for such. I do remember several large lidless wooden barrels in the room. Daddy stored his dried muskrat and mink pelts in these until the fur buyer (usually the land owner) made his next trip.

The dried skin on the pelts had a distinctive, permeating aroma not offensive to the trapping family depending upon them for livelihood, but which probably would have turned off most uplanders. Our family slept "among the pelts" almost every night of each four months marshland adventure and spent not a sleepless moment because of the smell. Now, more than 60 years later, I believe I would instantly recognize the aroma — and might even enjoy smelling it again.

Our family's trapping days ended the winter before I entered school. I do not know if school was the reason or if Daddy had tired of that hard life. As a first grader, I recall classmates who were absent the entire winter because they were at trapping grounds with their fathers. We could have managed, too. But Daddy sold the "Rhode Island" and the houseboat and our need for a home away from home was no more.

Grandma Was a Sailmaker

~3~

GRANDMA'S BREAD SNACK

Little boys get hungry often during the day. Their small-scale body engines need to be refueled with greater frequency than parents sometimes realize. Parents are often obsessed with the principle of three balanced meals a day and forget to more frequently oil and gas the constantly running little engines.

I was just such a little engine and my mother was one of the parents who did not believe in eating between meals. The result was that I made it pretty well from breakfast to lunch. That period always seemed shorter than from lunch to dinner (or supper, as we Cajuns like to call it).

But about midway through the afternoon my little engine began to sputter and cough for want of fuel and the rest of me slowed down considerably in velocity and efficiency. It was then that my eyes turned toward Grandma's house.

Grandma lived next door. By the time I first arrived on the scene, Grandpa had been dead 20 years and Grandma didn't help make sails anymore. So she concentrated on more womanly chores, one of which was baking homemade bread.

After first glancing over to Grandma's, I'd look over our place for a glimpse of Mother. If I saw her, I would announce that I was going over to visit Grandma

and hope that my pronouncement was not counter-
acted. If I didn't see her, which usually was the case
because Mother kept busy with household chores of
her own, I'd open the gate and in a half-dozen quick
steps would be safely inside Grandma's house.

I was too young to know much about how
Grandma made homemade bread. But I do know that
she made yeast cakes which I frequently saw drying in
pans on the front porch. And I know that the dough
went through a rising process because I remember
pans of it covered with damp cloths while Grandma
waited for it to do so. I recall also that she shaped the
dough into both long French loaves and round French
loaves.

What I remember most was the delicious aroma
which wafted throughout Grandma's house when she
was baking bread in her old wood-burning cast-iron
stove. It filled one's lungs with bliss and caused the
stomach to churn with desire.

Slipping over to Grandma's when my little engine was showing signs of wanting to quit on me
wasn't always easy. Nor was it always successful. But
when I did succeed it was like I imagined heaven to be!
Grandma wouldn't ask if I was hungry. She'd just pick
up one of the uncut round loaves and halve it cross-
wise, then cut a slice the whole width of the loaf. Why
she didn't cut from a partial loaf or one of the long
loaves, I never thought to ask.

Putting the bread knife down, Grandma walked
to the water bucket. She dipped a small amount of
water and, with the dipper, sprinkled it over the bread
slice lying on her outstretched hand. On to the sugar
container. She next carefully spooned sugar over the

entire slice of bread and handed it to me to enjoy. The taste was terrific! Better than bread and butter and jelly. We didn't have much of the latter two anyway when I was growing up. We had no cow and the fruits we grew were limited to figs, peaches, and Japanese plums.

It didn't take long for my little engine to rev up again. The sugar provided quick energy and the big, thick slice of bread was a real filler. Now I could go full-speed until I heard Mother's call to supper.

I know that on occasion Mother found out about my re-fueling at Grandma's. I don't recall the two of them having but a few words about it each time. Maybe Mother didn't really mind my having an indulgent grandmother. Maybe she didn't really mind my afternoon snacks. Maybe she personally didn't want to compromise her standards so if Grandma did it that absolved her of responsibility. I loved my grandma and it was times like these that told me she loved me, too.

Grandma Was a Sailmaker

~4~

JUST LIKE DAD

Our family's trapping days and nights were largely spent in a houseboat. We were either being towed by shrimp lugger to trapping grounds, moored alongside the marsh, or being towed back home. In the eyes of a small boy, the houseboat environment was confining. But the marsh was vast, interesting, and always beckoning.

My greatest desire at the time was to be a trapper and hunter like Daddy. I wanted to rise in the wee hours of each morning, collect the live duck decoys, and pole our pirogue to a secluded pond where wild mallards and pintails soon would be headed.

Decoys set out in the pond and each securely anchored by a string tied to one leg, Daddy and I would wait in hidden confidence in our blind constructed of marsh grass. At very first light the ducks would come— having heard our decoys calling. With folded wings, they would drop toward the decoys. Daddy and I would shoot with unerring aim while the ducks were still airborne.

After a very successful hunt, I wanted to join Daddy as he ran his trap lines meandering over the vast leased marsh. Secured and marked by a six or seven foot cane pole stuck through the ring at the end of its chain, each trap was a vise-like jaw which the trapper spread open and latched in position. To run the trap lines with Daddy would require that I help pole our pirogue through the tiny waterways in the marsh and check each trap to see if it had been set off.

If it had, whether empty or containing a musk-rat or mink, the trap must be reset. I would help Daddy until every trap in every line had been examined.

Once back at the houseboat, there would remain for us the tasks of skinning, placing pelts inside out on wire frames, and hanging these on racks to dry for several days in the sun. Yes, indeed! I wanted most to be a hunter and trapper like my dad.

Since I was too young to accompany Daddy while he hunted and ran his trap lines, my days were spent in the houseboat or in the clearing which separated it from the marsh. I owned few bought toys. Money was always scarce. I amused myself with toys fashioned out of paper scraps or wood. Sticks and a lively imagination made acceptable ponies and unerring guns. A longer stick was just the right support for pretending to walk the marsh while running my own trap lines. I was at once whatever I wished to be.

Sometimes what I wished to be or do did not coincide with Mother's version. She usually prevailed, but there was one morning when I furiously bounded out of the houseboat and ran away from home. Mother had been the cause of my displeasure. Of that I am sure, but I do not remember why. I hid behind Daddy's live duck decoy cage, determined to await his return from trapping before running farther away.

I do recall how Mother soon shamed me into giving up and returning to the houseboat. Leaning out of a window, she did not beg that I return. She didn't even ask me to. Showing no concern, she instead offered to bring my straw hat to protect me from the sun (the winter sun, yet!) during my journey away from home. Thus my rebellion was quickly and effectively crushed!

Grandma Was a Sailmaker

~5~

UNUSUAL CHRISTMAS EVE
AT BAYOU PEROT

Children have been excited on Christmas Eve since before Virginia wondered if there was a Santa Claus and wrote her now-famous letter to the New York Sun in 1897. Anticipation of the jolly little man's generosity could be read on tiny faces as easily as words on a school desk slate. Parents, too, shared the anticipation with their children. But there was one Christmas Eve during my childhood when our excitement switched from the anticipation of gifts to a desire for survival.

It was 1930, give or take a year. I was a preschooler running as fast as I could from within a stand of *roseau* (wild cane) growing near the edge of a clearing on the bank of Bayou Perot in either Lafourche or Jefferson Parish. I say either because Bayou Perot squiggles back and forth across the boundary between these adjoining parishes and I don't know exactly where Daddy's trapping lease was.

My destination was the houseboat tied to posts driven in the water's edge. And at the moment Christmas Eve wasn't even in my mind. As I reached the bank, my father walked down the plank suspended between the houseboat and shore. Father was a fur trapper in winter and a shrimp trawler the rest

17

of the year. The houseboat was our home from November through February.

"Daddy! Daddy! Come see what I caught!" I exclaimed. He followed me past his live duck decoy cage to where the cane grew. I proudly pushed aside the reeds to reveal a muskrat trap holding two dead muskrats caught by their tails!

To subdue my insistent demands that I be taken into the marsh to help run his trap line, Father had set in the cane reeds a trap which I could call my very own. Chances of catching anything there were nil, but Daddy had planned well. The muskrats in my trap secretly had been placed there when he returned with his daily catch.

My excitement was so great that the absurdity of catching two muskrats by the tail in the same trap, an action which certainly would not have resulted in their demise, never registered with me. And it did nothing but drive thoughts of Christmas Eve even farther from my mind.

As I passed the duck cage, I was not even reminded of the embarrassing time last winter when I had run away from home and hid behind it. Nor did the beauty and quacking of Dad's live mallard decoys serve to distract from my singleness of mind.

This day, I was so overwhelmed by my success at trapping that nothing, it seemed, would remind me that it was Christmas Eve. Christmas was not then the big, commercial celebration it is today. Parents observed the holiday for what it is— the birthday of Jesus. Our country was caught in the throes of the Great Depression and children expected relatively little in the way of gifts. Still, Santa managed an

18

appearance at our home every Christmas Eve, winters spent in the marsh not withstanding.

This Christmas Eve we spent with our trapper neighbors. A family with several children, they lived nearby in a large, one-room camp built on stilts. We were invited to come over after supper to *faire la veillée* (spend the evening). There were hot refreshments for all. Adults talked as they warded off the cold by huddling around the pot-bellied stove. Games occupied the children and activity kept us warm.

There was no Christmas tree to decorate so we strung pop corn and the adults tied the long strings from wall to wall. While enjoying the decorating, we were startled by several shotgun blasts. Pellets hit the camp. Our host quickly blew out the lantern, grabbed his shotgun, threw open the door, and poised to fire. After a long wait with no further shooting, he closed the door and re-lit the lantern.

"*Cést les sauvages*," (It is the savages) someone said, concluding it must be descendants of early marsh-dwelling Indians. It was known they resented the white man's intrusion on trapping grounds they still considered theirs. These lands now were lawfully owned by others who leased them yearly to trappers such as my father and our neighbor. In retrospect, the attackers probably sought not so much to injure as to frighten us into leaving.

Excitement and anticipation, though not the usual kind, had indeed been a part of our Christmas Eve. The gaity of our celebration ruined, our family waited well into the night before assuming the danger was over and returning to the houseboat. Awakening Christmas morning, I was relieved to discover Santa had not been scared away by *les sauvages*.

Grandma Was a Sailmaker

~6~

A BOUCHERIE
TO REMEMBER

"How would you like to have your own little pig?"
I was asked by one of my parents. We were visiting a
farmer in Cut Off whose yard was over-run by piglets.
Actually, it only seemed that way. The sow had given
birth to a very large litter. The piglets were everywhere— running, chasing, rolling, rooting, gobbling
every edible thing in sight. And I was doing my best
to keep them stirred up. I was having fun.

For a four-year-old country boy, the question
was like being asked if I wanted ice cream or a candy
bar. Piglets were not new to me. At Grandma's there
usually was a hog— sometimes two— being fattened
for a future boucherie. A favorite pastime of mine was
to climb the rungs of the pen until I could see over the
top rail, then watch the pigs as they ate voraciously or
wallowed in the mud. Never, however, had any hog
been mine.

I answered the question affirmatively and, after
being asked for assurance that I would feed and water
my pet properly, I was told to select the one I wanted.
I looked the litter over carefully— as if I had not already
taken notice of every marking and characteristic. My
choice was a black and white football of energy which

I earlier had tried but failed to catch.

The farmer, more skilled than I at handling pigs, caught my selection and deposited it into a gunny sack. The sack securely tied with string and the money having changed hands, we departed for home. Soon after our arrival, my piglet was turned loose in Grandma's pen, which really was on our side of the shared back yard, and I commenced my feeding and watering chores.

For months I fed and watered, fed and watered. I gave him every food scrap I could find. He ate potato peelings, vegetable trimmings, dinner plate left-overs, and whatever else could be found to combine with water into "hog slop". He consumed ears and ears of corn including the cobs.

The piglet became a small pig, then a large pig. He continued eating while everyone who saw him commented on how fine he was. The weather grew cooler and finally cold. By then my pig was bigger than big.

My parents told me one evening that many people from the neighborhood would be coming the next day to assist with the boucherie. Boucherie? Until then, it had not occurred to me that I had been given not really a pig of my own, but one to fatten for the killing.

Next morning people milled all around the back yard, making preparations. A distant relative used to the task had been selected to make the actual kill. His method was a hammer blow to the forehead. When the time came, I hid in the far side of Grandma's house and pressed my hands tightly against my ears.

~7~

ONCE UPON A RASH

Ordinarily I was not a sassy kid. Although years later, at age 13 or 14, an uncle told me I was. My troubles with him grew out of having ready responses to everything he said— rather typical behavior for the adolescent thinking he knows it all. Today, adults would call it having a "smart-mouth"— the antithesis of what is meant.

Neither Mother nor Daddy ever accused me of being sassy. The "Rules of the Household" were clear and usually firm, but I could voice my disagreement as long as I did it civilly. Usually that didn't change much. However, I had no doubt both parents loved me dearly, sought to shelter me, and believed that, through their particular kind of guidance, I would "amount to something" we all could be proud of.

There was a time when I was sassy, however. I was only five years old then and I was miserable. I didn't mean to be sassy. I itched. I itched wretchedly.

Sometime earlier I had developed a rash of big red blotches. A rash of big red blotches covering practically all of my body. It itched. But in a few days it was gone. Then, in a week or so, another rash appeared. And it itched as much as the first one.

Our little community of Cote Blanche was not exactly blessed with an abundance of medical personnel or facilities. We didn't have a dentist. We didn't have a drug store. We did have one general practioner medical doctor who dispensed medications from his satchel or his office. After my rash had played hide and seek a few times, I finally was taken to old Doc Lemkowitz. This was no great undertaking since he lived just a few houses up the road. Diagnosis must have been a great accomplishment, however, for there were no tests to be run to identify the rash and no lab to run them in had the tests existed.

Doc must have known his business. He diagnosed the rash as due to eating pork and, for years thereafter, whenever I did the rash appeared. On this occasion he dispensed a blue medicated soap with which to lather the body and cover the blotches. That would stop the itch, he said, and the rash would gradually disappear— until the next time I ate pork.

Why I continued to eat pork I don't know, unless it was because it and chicken were our meat staples. We owned no cattle, so beef didn't grace our table too often. But we did raise pigs and chickens.

On the occasion of the particular outbreak around which this story centers, Mama and Papa and I were in the kitchen. It was after nightfall and illumination was provided by a single kerosene lamp resting on the kitchen table. We would not have electricity in our home until the following year. Daddy sat in his rocker, occupied with something on his lap. Mother sat in her rocker reading *True Confessions* magazine. I sat in a chair at the table playing with some toy.

The rash began to appear and I began to itch. As the rash grew worse, so did the itching. I turned to

Mother and informed her of what was happening. She replied that she would lather the rash with the medicated soap as soon as she finished the particular article she was reading.

I tried to wait patiently. But I itched. I really itched. I drew Mother's attention again. She replied as before that she'd tend to me soon and added the direction that I was to strip down and stand on the table.

I did as directed. And I continued to itch. And she continued to read. I really itched. I itched wretchedly. Finally, out of frustration and desperation, I shouted to Mother, "You don't care about me! You like that old magazine more than you do me!"

The magazine flew out of her hand to the floor. In a step or two she was at the table. Her hands flailed at my buttocks, delivering stinging slap after stinging slap. Standing there buck naked, I was completely defenseless and I did the only thing I could have. I cried.

Her anger vented, Mother picked up the medicated soap, wet it, and lathered over my rash. Then she wiped my tears and hugged me.

Grandma Was a Sailmaker

~8~

OF INNERTUBES AND TEARS

I recently had turned six. I would start school in the fall. Boys of my generation, at least those of Cajun decent who had "grown" to that age, were strongly discouraged from expression of emotion by way of tears.

To cry was to fall short of the "little man" image— the conditioned, strong, mature, male response sought by adults in their boy children. Whatever the cost, all weak or more feminine emotions such as crying were to be suppressed. I cried.

It was election day. We did not have yet our first family automobile. Daddy was to earn that some three years later as a bonus for selling more than all other door-to-door salesmen of Zanol products (notions, toiletries, etc.). The car was a Ford Model B and it came without bumpers. That doesn't have anything to do with what I'm telling you about except that it is something which has stuck in my mind all these years. I always have thought it was cheap to give away a car without bumpers!

Election days were important to our family. The times were those in which Huey Long ruled Louisiana politics upward to Washington from the state capitol and downward to the local courthouse. Every vote was either for "the machine" or against it. Daddy was a firm believer in the dishonesty of machine politics. Consequently, he and Mama accepted the offer of an automobile ride to the polling (voting) place, some miles away. There, strengthened by having to pay an ill-affordable poll tax to exercise the voting rights granted each of them by the Constitution, I feel certain they voted for every anti-Long candidate on the ballot.

I was left at home in the care of our neighbor, a kind, generous, caring uncle whom I grew to admire, love, respect, and today view as the finest man I have known. But not that day! Oh, he looked after me well. He was careful that I got into no trouble, was never in danger, and allowed me to dog his steps as he went about our common back yard doing chores.

I tagged along, step after step after step, my arm protruding through a discarded automobile inner-tube slung over my right shoulder. My prize possession! Where it came from I no longer remember. Since we had no car, I suspect Daddy had obtained it for me from someone who was about to discard it as useless. That innertube was so dear to this six-year old that in my mind it had taken on the characteristics of a human playmate. I was careful to keep it clean (How clean can a discarded innertube be?), to let it not out of touch and, above all, to keep it from all harm. I had projected unto that innertube the deep feeling which one playmate can develop for another.

A third cousin from down the road came over to play. My world soon shattered. Seeing my handsome possession, he asked for a piece. Innertubes did make the very best elastics for slingshots! And no self-respecting Cajun boy would be without a ready slingshot in his hip pocket. Even then I could feel mine nudging against my buttocks. It just happened, Cousin said, that one elastic on his was broken and needed replacing.

Now, an innertube is like an angel food cake. Once you cut a wedge out of it, no amount of pushing together will rejoin the resulting ends. I said no. My cousin did not complain or offer to fight or threaten to go home. Instead he went straight to my uncle, who had eluded us by continuing his chores as we stopped to hold our brief conversation.

His plea fell on sympathetic ears. Uncle came over to where I still stood and asked that I give up part of my innertube for cousin. I refused. He expressed disappointment at what he termed selfishness. I was taken aback. He just did not understand. My cousin did not understand. But selfish? Never! I surrendered the innertube.

As Uncle cut a sizeable wedge with his pocket knife and gave it to my cousin, tears welled up inside me. Cousin left to make his slingshot repairs and Uncle handed me the crescent which was left of my inner-tube. He was returning my friend! This mutilated thing was my friend! This thing sacrificed on the altar of shame was my friend! The tears burst forth and ran in torrents.

Uncle did his best to console me. He tried again and again, but the more effort he expended, the more tears were triggered. In desperation, I am sure, he resumed his chores and I resumed dogging his every step. Still the tears flowed, interrupted only by breath-taking whimpers.

Cousin, who had departed not unknowing of my

deep hurt, returned later to make a peace offering of the wedge of innertube— minus two strips now adorning his slingshot. What crassness! How could he believe that two pieces side-by-side would restore my friend to wholeness? How could he expect that I could erase the pain my friend had suffered, not to mention my own?

I declined even to touch his revolting offering and he left once more, slingshot protruding from one hip pocket and innertube piece from the other.

~9~

TEA COOKIES APLENTY!

As a youngster whenever I walked into Grandma's house and saw a couple of large, empty, lard cans setting on the floor, I knew what was about to happen. Most folks who didn't butcher on their own bought lard in multi-pound tins with resealable tops. The lard used, these cans usually were saved for storing other things.

At Grandma's, hogs were butchered during cool weather so she didn't buy lard. Her tins had come from some other source. Donated probably by someone having found little use for them, grandma's tins were filled with what I viewed as more precious than lard— tea cookies.

The pair of empty lard cans was a sure sign that Grandma was about to fire up her cast-iron wood stove— the same stove in which she so often baked mouth-watering sweet potatoes. I can still taste those red delicacies with skin unwrapped, split vertically down the middle and flavored with a pat of homemade butter, but they are not part of this story.

This time, grandma was preparing to bake dozens and dozens of round tea cookies— enough to fill both cans to the brim, and then some. The excess was to be consumed or shared with others during the next few days. The loaded tins would provide grandma's family with enough cookies to last several months.

31

Then the procedure would be repeated.

Grandma's tea cookie recipe has been pre-served by my cousin, Enosia Gaspard Savoie, who was reared by grandma. She refers to them as "Pillow Slip Cookies" because, for quick access, Grandma kept some in a clean white pillow case tied with a string and hung on a nail in the kitchen. The recipe calls for:

1 3/4 cups sugar	3 1/2 cups flour
1 cup shortening	1 pinch of salt
3 eggs	3 teaspoons baking powder
1 tablespoon vanilla extract	

Cream sugar and shortening. Add eggs and vanilla extract. Mix flour, baking powder, and salt, then add gradually to creamed ingredients. Roll out to 1/2 inch thickness and cut into desired size and shape. Bake.

In Grandma's lifetime thermostats on stoves were unknown. How long to bake was a matter of judgement based on how hot the woodstove oven was and how brown one wanted the cookies. Grandma had a favorite colloquial expression to cover this. "*Faire cuire a la couleur de l'esprit*" (bake to the color of the spirit) meant she liked her cookies to be on the light side. Today, this could be attained by baking 10-12 minutes at 350 degrees.

Grandma's cookie baking was always special with the children of the neighborhood. Her products were sweet and tasty and they kept well. Not that longevity was a matter of importance to us. In addition to the round ones, every baking yielded cookies shaped like boys and girls with out-stretched hands and feet— scarecrow style. These were for immediate consumption, hot out of the oven, compliments of a caring grandmother and neighbor.

~10~

SITTING ON THE FREEZER

"Come in the back yard and play," the small voice said.

"I can't," I replied.

"Come on. We'll play hide and seek or marbles or cowboys and Indians," pleaded the small voice which was that of my cousin Stephen. He and a near half-dozen other children of the neighborhood awaited my reply.

"I can't," I repeated. "I'm sitting on the freezer."

Sitting on the ice cream freezer was a favorite summer pastime for the children congregating with their parents each Sunday afternoon at Grandma's. Sunday afternoon ice cream at Grandma's usually was a two freezer affair. Not that there were ever two freezers in operation. Such a luxury as an ice cream freezer was hard to come by, but sufficient have-nots of the neighborhood congregated with the haves to necessitate freezing two different batches. So, the one freezer did double duty. Always one freezerfull was chocolate and the other vanilla.

There was competition among us for the right to sit upon a couple of folded oyster sacks atop the freezer as the adult men took turns handcranking. Asking first was not the only criteria for being selected.

One had to be heavy enough to keep the freezer from moving when the cranking got tough. Being pudgy aided my cause and resulted in my being chosen for the honor more than any other child.

Why would I give up games of hide and seek or marbles to sit on a freezer while the other children played? Simple.

When the freezing was complete, the dasher with all clinging ice cream belonged to the sitter. Sitting there was a marvelous time of anticipation.

First the freezer was tilted and the brine poured out. Then the freezer was allowed to "rest" for some 30 minutes while the ice cream hardened. Finally, the cranking mechanism was removed and the container with the ice cream lifted out. A careful twist and the cover was off, revealing the delicious cream, home-prepared by Grandma and the other ladies.

A hardy yank and out came the dasher with gobs of mouth-watering ice cream clinging to it. This was set in a bowl and handed over with spoon to the freezer sitter. A just reward for sacrifices endured.

~11~

PADDLE WHEELERS ON THE BAYOU

Bayou Lafourche was dammed from the Mississippi River in 1903. For many years I thoughtlessly believed this flood control measure had been constructed in the late 1930's. What caused me to think so were the memories of rear paddle wheel boats cruising up and down the bayou at Cote Blanche, where we lived. I had supposed these boats, used to transport goods from wholesalers to the general mercantile stores along the bayou, were loaded with their supplies in New Orleans. Then followed the up-river trip to the source of Bayou Lafourche at Donaldsonville. Finally the boats had steamed down the bayou as far as Golden Meadow, unloading at every general mercantile store along the way.

Not so! When I watched these intriguing boats in action in the late 1920's and early 1930's, the bayou had already been dammed for two decades. The boats, carrying kegs of syrup and sacks of flour, sugar, beans, and rice numbering in the hundreds, could not have entered Bayou Lafourche at Donaldsonville.

As I thought, New Orleans was the shipping point. But there were different routes available to get the goods to the Bayou. One, a main line rail road, ran from New Orleans through Raceland on its way westward, as it still does. A spur line ran southeast to

Lockport. Goods made their way to some boats over this route. In return, farmers shipped potatoes and onions by paddle wheeler to the railhead for transfer to rail cars going north.

An all-water route was from the Crescent City through Bayou Segnette, skirting the north shore across Lake Salvador, thence by the Company Canal and through the locks at Lockport. This probably was longer but safer than coming out of Bayou Segnette, crossing the middle of Lake Salvador, and traveling the Harang Canal to Larose. Another option for both water routes was to travel Bayou Barataria rather than Bayou Segnette. In 1900 the canal for which Cut Off was named was dug and briefly provided yet another route to New Orleans.

There were at least six different stern wheelers which plied their trade in Bayou Lafourche during my growing years. My favorite was the "Gem", owned by a family named Callais.

What made me feel special toward it was that, between runs, the "Gem" was moored a mile or two to the south. This made it one of ours— a "Cajun paddle boat", so to speak. It is said that a predecessor to the "Gem", owned by the same family, was pulled onto the ways (a colloquial expression for a timber framework on which a boat is built or repaired and along which it slides in launching), broke the ways, and sank.

Other stern wheelers operating at the same time as the "Gem" were the "F. T. Nicholls" and "Percy Lobdell" owned by the Percy Lobdell Wholesale Company of Lockport, the "Laura Ann" owned by Milton Egle of Golden Meadow, and the "Naccari". Egle sold gasoline to shrimp boats and his paddle wheeler was used chiefly for transporting that.

My vantage point for watching steamboats was a good one. Sitting on the levee was a way of passing time which everyone could enjoy. But I was fortunate enough to live two houses down (less than 100 feet) from Ernest Gaspard's General Mercantile Store. I could sit on the levee in front of our house, clasp my knees in my arms, and watch the entertaining activity of Mr. Gaspard's merchandise being unloaded. Others did the same at the general mercantile stores of Elie Ducos and Wilson Petit at Cut Off, John Guidry at Galliano, and Marc Picciola, Daize Cheramie, Joe Perrin, John Lafont, and Leon Theriot at Golden Meadow.

On-lookers were called to the bayouside by several short blasts of the steamboat's throaty whistle. This really was done to alert the storekeeper to the impending unloading of his goods, but it served more as an excitement to the children and adults of the neighborhood.

There was no wharf or pier for the steamboats to tie on to. As a boat approached the bank, a considerable amount of maneuvering was necessary to get close enough. This meant putting the boat in reverse and forward and reverse and forward again several times, each time with an accompanying giant "swoosh" of water churned by the paddle wheel and a burst of black smoke from the twin stacks.

When the captain had succeeded in manuevering his vessel to within some 10 feet of the shore, deckhands shoved a long board landward until it strattled the open water between boat and shore. Then commenced the most entertaining part of the unloading operation.

Deckhands, most of whom were big, tall black men and all of whom had large rippling muscles, picked up the 100 pound sacks or kegs of syrup one at a time. Mr. Edgar Pierce, a resident of the area, called the kegs "barrels of dirty faces" because children would later eat the syrup and go around with sticky, dirty faces.

Swinging his load to a shoulder, each deckhand walked the plank. Every step caused the plank, which was a foot wide and three or four inches thick, to wobble up and down, up and down as if it were a trampoline. It was exciting to watch and daring to wonder if the plank would break. It never did.

Unloading completed, the deckhands retrieved the plank and the steamboat paddle wheel began a furious backward rotation which made the bayou water seem like that at the foot of Niagra Falls. The stacks belched mouthful after mouthfull of thick, black smoke until the boat slowly pulled from shore. In deeper water the boat captain signaled for the paddle wheel to turn forward and the vessel resumed its voyage downstream. A final toot of the whistle said, "Goodbye until next trip."

Grandma Was a Sailmaker

~12~

EARLY ADVENTURE

As a young child hardly of school age, I well remember frolicking on the Fourchon beach during what was quite an adventure for my cousin Stephen and me.

His father, Paul Lefort, Jr., was a commercial fisherman who had recently begun a building materials sideline. The concrete pillars which he sold for Cajun houses were made by him using free bayou water, bought cement and gravel, and free sand hauled from Fourchon beach— a perfectly legal action at the time.

During one summer vacation from school, my cousin and I were invited on a sand procurement boat trip. There was no road even nearing Fourchon then and, equally distressing, there was no truck available to us had there been a road. Locally owned motorized vehicles were rather scarce then on Bayou Lafourche and most of those seen were Model T or Model A Ford cars. The trip would be a fun excursion for us. The only stipulation was that we hold open the sacks into which the men were to shovel sand. To this we readily agreed.

Long before dawn the following morning, we left in the shrimp lugger belonging to Stephen's father.

Grandma Was a Sailmaker

Despite it being summertime, early morning over the water was cold. Stephen and I huddled in the cabin, alternately peeking out at the galaxies and glancing at the red-hot manifold of the boat engine. We were apprehensive of the glow, the only illumination except for the boat's red and green running lights. At the same time, we were grateful for the warmth.

After what seemed a very long trip, we arrived at Fourchon and anchored within the western fork of Bayou Lafourche at its intersection with the Gulf of Mexico. First came breakfast, then filling of the sand bags. Mr. Lefort and his hired hand, Oscar Gaspard, shoveled dry sand into gunny sacks while Stephen and I held them open. The shoveling was hard, muscle-aching work and there was a rest period whenever either man tired. Stephen and I also welcomed these breaks from our duties. They provided us with opportunities to scurry to the water's edge to wet our bare feet in the surf.

When all the sacks were filled, there remained for the men the heavy loading of these into the boat's hold. Stephen and I, however, were free to roam the beach. We relished the salty smell and taste of the gulf as we looked for seashells, odd pieces of driftwood, and other curiosities. As we walked on the wet sand near the water's edge, our feet left mushy imprints like elongated saucers quickly filling with brine. Our toes dug into the dry loose sand as we visually combed areas where previous high tides could have deposited small boy treasures. We wondered about far-away shores and big ships from which these treasures might have come.

Whatever we found of sufficient interest to keep, Stephen and I stuffed into pockets until all were puffed like the cheeks of a blowfish. Straw hats came off to accommodate more findings and, when these could hold no more, a secluded corner of the boat cabin became our depository. It was this day that I first saw stone crabs and the amusing fiddler crabs which run sideways on the tips of their claws, then dart into burrows in the sand.

Mid-afternoon arrived before the boat was fully loaded. Men and boys of the crew devoured a decidedly late lunch. Before entering the cabin for the long journey home, Stephen and I cast long, wistful glances at our newly discovered "Treasure Island", wondering if ever again we would set foot on its exciting shore. Within minutes, two very tired boys were fast asleep and neither awoke until the boat docked well into the night.

Grandma Was a Sailmaker

~13~

A GIFT AT CHRISTMAS

I watched my classmate curiously as we stood aboard the school ferry. It was the next-to-last morning before school closed for the Christmas holidays. We were first graders being transported from "our side" of the bayou to the school side.

In addition to his Bob And Nancy reader and blue-back speller, my classmate carried three Christmas presents to be placed under our classroom tree. It was strange to see him loaded down with this many gifts. His family was far from being "well off". Ours wasn't either. This was 1932, the Great Depression. Franklin Roosevelt had been elected president less than two months earlier and would not take office until March 9, 1933. His programs for relieving unemployment, helping the farmers, and balancing the budget were still to come. While we Wetlands Cajuns did not want for food to eat, money was scarce— extremely scarce.

As I looked at my classmate with his armful of gifts, I could not help noticing that he was dressed as usual— rather shabbily. His dark pants were worn at the knees and his coat was an obvious hand-me-down at least two sizes too big. Even his cap had a dull, battered look. But his grin was wide and he seemed in a festive mood.

Grandma Was a Sailmaker

I half-hid behind my books the two small presents I was carrying. One was for the name I had drawn for the present exchange and the other was for my best friend, also a classmate. These paled in comparison to the three gifts prominently in view across from me. "Whom are those for?" I asked.

"This one is for the name I drew," he replied. "And this one for..." He proceeded to name a classmate, then concluded with, "...and this one is for you."

My heart jumped— and sank— at the same time. He and I never had been close. Yet, he had a gift for me. And I had not one for him.

When I arrived home that afternoon, Mother was at the galvanized tin sink in the kitchen, washing Irish potatoes which would be part of our supper. She dried her hands and we sat at our small dinner table while she asked about my day at school. I related the incident about the gift.

I would not have described Mother's size as slight. Neither was her sense of what was proper. A white hand brushed back her black hair and she said, "You must give him something."

Mother arose and, after searching the house to locate a few coins, soon departed for the neighborhood general mercantile store. When she returned, she held a roman candle. We wrapped the gift and placed it with my school things.

Next morning I carefully clutched the tubular package as we ferried across. My classmate eyed me carefully, but said nothing about what I carried. I said nothing either.

That afternoon, when school work was over and the teacher had passed out cookies and home-made root beer, the distribution of presents began. She picked up one gift at a time from under the tree, reading each name carefully before handing it to the recipient. One of the first gifts distributed was the tubular package I had brought. My classmate went to the front of the class when his name was called, then strolled back clutching the package and showing a wide toothy grin, the whiteness of which contrasted sharply with the darkness of his hair.

My first gift was from my best friend—a nice Lotto game, similar to what is known in south Louisiana as Keeno. The second gift I received was from the person who had drawn my name. I don't remember what that was—perhaps because of my great and mounting anticipation for my other gift. The number of undelivered gifts dwindled until there was but one. I readied myself for a hurried walk from my desk to the tree to claim what I knew was mine.

Teacher's voice called out the name and it was not mine! I was shocked! I had been swindled! Feeling foolish, I said nothing. That afternoon as the ferry carried us to "our side" of the bayou, my enterprising classmate avoided conversations, but in his arms he held more gifts than anyone else.

Grandma Was a Sailmaker

~14~

A MATTER OF FAITH

I think of myself as having been reared, for the most part, by my mother. Not that Daddy wasn't there. Except for my earliest childhood, when he was a shrimp trawler, he was home every night. But that's it. He was home at night and seldom during the day, so the decisions of parenthood fell to or were appropriated by Mother.

I never thought of Mother as indecisive. With her, things seemed to be largely black or white, seldom gray. She acted usually with swiftness and determination, convinced that few persons achieve because they are destined to, but most because they are determined to. I see much of her in me.

In retrospect, Mother was not an easy mother to be reared by. She kept a close reign on me— too close, I felt at times. She demanded much in the way of my meeting her standards. Scholarship, conduct, dress, church were all important. Her faith in God was absolute.

Mother never read Dean Walley's charmingly illustrated 1971 book, **Pathways to Faith**. Had she, she would have agreed that "As the sun nourishes the earth, the light of faith can nourish our lives and help us grow closer to the Source of life. As the moon pulls the tides, the power of faith can cause our lives to flow out of oceans of turbulence and fear toward quiet harbors of serenity."

Mother's faith and Daddy's, which was not expressed as vocally, resulted in two early experiences in my life which left me convinced that faith healing should not be taken lightly. The first occurred when I was more than three and a half, but not yet of school age.

I suffered— and that is the correct word— from a chronic case of enuresis or bed-wetting. I am sure Mother and Daddy suffered, too. I think even now about how unpleasant her every morning chore of stripping wet linens off the bed and washing these must have been. Protecting the mattress with rubber sheeting and absorbent pads made the task a little easier, but no more pleasant.

The medical community today states enuresis, especially when occurring after a long period of dryness (which was not my case), can be psychological in nature. But it also admits that, in most cases, the cause is unknown. Following the theory of treating cause to remove effect, then, leaves one no better off medically today than I was in the 1920's. And thus it was that my parents trusted in faith— their faith— and sought out a *traiteur* or faith healer.

They learned of one in Labadieville, some fifty miles north of where we lived. We drove there on a Sunday afternoon. The house was Cajun in style, old, and unpainted. Every window opening was closed with heavy wooden shutter, as if the house were deserted.

Daddy knocked on a side door. He knocked

again. The door slowly swung partially open and a thin, very old black man stood there. Daddy and he spoke. I could not hear what was said, but soon Daddy motioned for Mother and me to come.

The old man waited until we arrived at the steps. He motioned for me to come in, but Mother and Daddy to remain outside. We entered into a large dark room, the only light in which came from the open doorway. I was reminded of the similar room in Grandma's Cajun house where meals were cooked and eaten and folks sat around the fireplace on winter nights. But hers was well lit.

In the middle of this man's room was a large, bare table with several chairs around it. Striking a match, the old man lit a candle and placed it on the table. For the first time I could see other pieces of furniture placed against the walls. He sat in a chair before the candle and motioned me to approach. He told me to lower my trousers and underwear slightly to reveal the bladder area of my abdomen.

This done, the old man began a series of incantations which I did not understand. With right hand closed except for his extended thumb, he periodically passed the thumb through the candle flame. After each such movement, he gently touched me in a sweeping motion across the bladder area while continuing his chanting.

After some minutes of this I was told to pull up my clothing and he led me outside where my parents stood. Words I don't remember were exchanged between them. I do remember that I was never again bothered by enuresis.

The second experience occurred much later—

when I was in school vacation, probably between grades eight and nine. That summer I was traveling almost daily with Daddy while he drove his routes as salesman for Itzkovitch Furniture Company of New Orleans. He was gradually teaching me to drive and, like every fourteen-year-old even to this day, I was eager to accompany him for that reason.

A small ringworm (Tinea) had developed in the middle of my back some weeks earlier. The medical community identifies ringworm as a fungus which infects the skin and causes scaly, round, itchy patches to develop. Ringworm on the trunk starts as a small, round, red patch and is said to gradually grow bigger until it is about one inch across. As it gets bigger, the central area heals and leaves a red ring on the skin.

My ringworm didn't stop spreading at one inch. It grew larger and larger until, by mid-summer, it reached from shoulders to waist and equally far from side-to-side. One day as we traveled north on the east side of Bayou Lafourche, Daddy suddenly slowed the car and pointed to one of a pair of small white houses. A man in undershirt and trousers rocked on the porch.

"That's Mr._____(Daddy called some name I long since have lost from memory). He's a *traiteur*."

The car gentled to a halt. We climbed out, entered the man's yard, and walked up to the porch. Daddy introduced us and told the man I had a ringworm which needed treatment. As we stood in the yard and he continued to sit in his rocker, the man told me to remove my shirt and to turn around. I did as he requested.

Facing away from him, I could not see what the

man did. I know he neither left his rocker nor touched me. I did not hear him incant aloud. After a few minutes he told me to put my shirt on again. We thanked him for his healing efforts and resumed our travel. Within a few days the red hue of the ringworm diminished. It gradually turned brown and in a week had vanished completely.

Faith healing is a controversial subject today, but it was common practice during the days of my ancestors and as I grew up. I do not profess to have much knowledge about it except for these two personal experiences. Neither can I claim that the healings which took place for me did so because of my faith. In both instances I could be described as faith-neutral. I really didn't know enough to believe or to question the practice. My parents did have faith, however, and the ability to act decisively.

Grandma Was a Sailmaker

~15~

TRACKS INTO FRIENDSHIP

By the time I was in the first grade, my father had gone from shrimper/trapper to selling Zanol Products (notions) to selling burial insurance. Now he added a second line— route furniture salesman for Itzkovitch Furniture Company of New Orleans.

His route took him from Golden Meadow north to Raceland on both sides of Bayou Lafourche and would prove so successful that in a short time he could give up the insurance sales. A condition of his newest employment was that he motor to New Orleans once a month for an audit of his records. He did this from 1932 until he opened a business of his own in 1945.

When it was monthly audit time, he and Mother would leave soon after daybreak in the Ford automobile he had won as top Zanol salesman. This was always a school day for me. School busses would not make their appearance at our school until some 10 years later, so my parents arranged to drop me off at an early-rising family's residence located on our side of the bayou a short distance from the school ferry. There I was to wait until it was time to walk to the ferry and cross to school.

The family's home was an impressive, white, two-story house of many rooms set on large grounds.

Besides the parents, there were six or seven children. Nearest my age was the youngest— a boy of 10 named Elmo Authement.

Either by process of elimination or by parental decree, it befell this 10-year-old to be my host. I now can visualize how thrilled he must have been to have a six-year-old dog his every footstep as he went about his morning chores, which included milking two cows. Must have been a real joy for him— especially if witnessed by one of his peers who happened to be heading for the school ferry early.

My monthly event there began usually with his mother's offer of a cup of milk, sometimes more. There was no doubt I was too young to be offered coffee. She couldn't have known that my every school morning breakfast consisted of a cup of *café au lait* (coffee milk) crammed full of corn flakes and topped with cream from boiled milk.

As Elmo left through the back door to begin his chores, I followed as close behind as I could manage. Usually that was not difficult. He mostly didn't walk too fast. Should he suddenly turn the corner of some farm building, his footsteps would be clearly marked in the heavy dew of the morning.

I do not recall any special conversations which we had. Nor do I remember how long I was thrust upon this boy. It had to be several years before my parents saw me as old enough to be delivered at the ferry landing shortly after dawn.

As the arrangement continued, our friendship developed a hidden strength which was not to surface for many years. Maybe it was a big brother-little brother sort of relationship— tolerance and pranks on one hand, admiration and doggedness on the other. It wasn't because we did other things together. And we seldom saw one another even on our school campus.

We lost touch after he went to college in 1939. We didn't make contact when we both served in World War II and he, again, in the Korean War. Later, I learned he was living in the Lafayette area. In 1963 he showed up on the faculty of the university where I had been teaching since 1957. Our friendship resumed...as if our boyhood tracks in the dew had never dried.

Grandma Was a Sailmaker

~16~

"CRACK!" SAID THE WHIP

"Crack!" said the whip. "Crack!" The sound echoed through the neighborhood.

The young man from Larose coiled the long bullwhip, a full-size cattle persuader, and handed it to me. I beamed with joy, thanked him excitedly, and made my way to our house next door. The whip was heavy. It was made of cured rawhide strips woven on a stout wooden handle at one end and tapered into a cat-of-nine tails at the other. The smell of the rawhide was distinctive and akin to that of the dried pelts Daddy stored in barrels when he was a trapper.

It was dusk; no, past dusk. Sufficient darkness had set in to erase completely all except the very final vestige of light. I looked back the fifty feet toward where the young man, Luke Savoie, stood with his fiance, my cousin Enosia Gaspard, next to the front steps of Grandma's house. I could no longer distinguish their forms.

In the days and weeks and months which followed, I countless times climbed astride the banister surrounding our front porch. It was just the right height to simulate a horse, especially with a makeshift rope bridle tied thereon. The long rawhide whip dangled from my right hand and, as I rode the imaginary range like a seasoned vaccaro, I cracked the whip to bunch the herd.

I first met Luke in the 1930's when he came to court "No-No," as every-one called cousin. I was about six, maybe seven. Each time he came we exchanged greetings, but not much more. Mama was always careful that I not linger on the scene so as not to interfere with their courtship.

When he arrived for one such summer evening visit, I was astride our banister riding my imaginary steed of the western range. In my hand was a two foot length of broomstick with a piece of rope or heavy string tied thereon. I popped my homemade "whip" and produced only an imaginary sound.

Luke eyed my plight and said, "How would you like to have a real whip— one made of rawhide that really cracks?"

I was unable to find the words to respond. "I'll get the butcher in Larose to make one for you," he continued, "and I'll bring it when I come back."

So it was that the young man next appeared at dusk of a day about one week later, coiled rawhide whip in hand. He called me from our yard and started to hand me the whip, then retreated. "Let me show you how to pop it," said he, as he slightly backed away from the front steps of Grandma's house.

"Crack!" said the whip. "Crack!" The sound echoed through the neighborhood.

Next morning Grandmother went unto the front porch to contemplate her beautiful flowers in beds near the steps. Every flower was cut to the ground, victim of the cat-of- nine-tails at the end of my whip.

~20~

35¢ CATFISH

When I was growing up my paternal grandfather, Maximillien Pitre, lived in Golden Meadow, a few miles south of us. This was not the grandfather who made sails, but he had been a fisherman and had started off most of his sons, including my father, learning the same trade. None but Daddy stayed in it very long. There were easier ways to make a living even then. And Daddy, too, eventually would sell his boat and turn to merchandising.

I suppose Grandpa always kept a love for the water. Even after he retired and sold his boat, he continued to live in the fishing community that Golden Meadow was back then. His house was just across the roadway from the bayou and he could see boats navigating up and down, up and down.

Grandpa had a large family when Grandma died shortly after the birth of their youngest child, who was six years older than me. Grandpa's oldest daughter took over the rearing of her siblings and refused to marry until well after all the others had and were gone from the family home.

It was in the earlier years that I remember Grandpa periodically coming to Cote Blanche to visit with us for a few days. He didn't have an automobile and wouldn't have known how to drive it even if he had. We did, Daddy having won a Model B Ford for outstanding salesmanship. So it befell Daddy to go for Grandpa and to return him when Grandpa figured he'd stayed long enough— which usually was about a week. On one such visit, Grandpa took me fishing from the bank of Bayou Lafourche the afternoon he was to return home. The bayou flowed in front of where we lived, but I didn't fish often because I wasn't allowed to go near the water without adult supervision. So fishing was a grand treat for this little Cajun boy.

We gathered a pair of cane poles from Daddy's garage or my next-door uncle's barn and attached lines, bobbers, and hooks. For bait we prepared a stiff

62

dough in anticipation of catching catfish. Worms dug from moist earth were the usual bait for bayou fishing when in search of blue gills or other of the perch family. But Grandpa was an experienced fisherman and he said catfish bit best on dough.

At the bayou side we baited hooks, threw in our lines and prepared to out-wait the catfish. Grandpa sat on the bank and stretched his long legs. I didn't get to sit down. My bobber suddenly disappeared but I wasn't looking.

Grandpa yelled, "Pull it up! Pull it up!" I yanked the taunt line from the water and out came a wriggling catfish smaller than what my youthful eyes perceived. But it was a keeper. I baited the hook again and cast the line back into the water.

You never saw such a procession as had begun! Catfish after catfish bit my line and catfish after catfish wound up in the bucket we'd brought along. Grandpa's bobber seldom went under, but mine played hide and seek for the entire time we fished. And I missed very few opportunities to land a fish. I had never seen such a collection of catfish before.

Too soon it was time for Grandpa to head home. He suggested that we take the fish along and sell them at a fish market in Golden Meadow. I readily agreed. When we arrived there, Grandpa handled the transaction while Daddy and I waited near the car. Soon he returned, asked for my hand, and dribbled 35¢ into it.

35¢! 35¢! I was ecstatic! I had never possessed this much money before. I felt like a Rockefeller (though I feel sure I had no idea who or what that was). A field worker earned at most $1.00 a day and I owned 35¢!

~18~

CHICKEN, ANYONE?

If I were to ask any one of my grandchildren where to go for a chicken to cook, the answer most assuredly would be "To the supermarket, Pa-paw."

Should I show doubt as to the wisdom of this advice, he or she could point to this week's grocery ads in the local newspaper and find words and graphics proclaiming, "Fresh Fryers, 59¢/lb." and "Baking Hens, 69¢/lb."—dressed, of course.

My grandchild would be correct, but it wasn't always that way. In fact, it wasn't that way long after I was much older than my grandchild's age. My mother never bought a dressed chicken until after World War II and I don't believe Grandma ever bought a dressed chicken at all.

This doesn't mean we didn't have chicken to eat. They just came out of the barnyard instead of a store. During my childhood, we bought groceries from general mercantile stores which had little refrigeration. Meat was purchased from a butcher shop, the proprietor of which did his own slaughtering and dressing of beef and pork, but shied away from handling poultry. Perhaps it was because almost all families in our community raised chickens while few were equipped for cattle, other than a milk cow.

For several years the chicken-raising for our

family was one of Grandma's undertakings—until I became old enough to assume charge of that and the vegetable garden. Since we raised chickens for both eggs and meat, we largely stayed with Plymouth Barred Rocks and Rhode Island Reds—both good producers of each. The younger hens were allowed to lay and those past their prime became fare for the stewpot.

Because of arthritic knees, Grandma needed assistance in capturing chickens to be cooked. She would recruit someone to capture the desired hen and bring it to her. Without ceremony she would wring the chicken's neck and fling it to the ground where it fluttered momentarily. The capturer then would hand Grandma the dead chicken. A few hours later, Grandma had plucked and dressed the hen and the delicious aroma of chicken stew wafted from her house.

I remember an occasion when I, being the capturer, brought the chicken to Grandma. She wrung the neck and flung the hen to the ground as usual. The bird fluttered once, then quickly got up and ran off before spreading its none-too-strong wings and flying onto the roof of Grandma's house.

Faced with a dilemma, Grandma directed that I throw pieces of dried mud at the chicken. I scored no direct hits and few near-misses. My only success was in driving the hen to the peak of the roof. By then I could envision chicken stew without chicken. But Grandma had not exhausted her resourcefulness. She sent me next door to our house to bring Daddy back.

Daddy saw the situation and returned home

briefly. He soon re-appeared with his twelve gauge shotgun. A single shot dispatched the hen and before long Grandma was plucking and dressing the main ingredient in her next chicken stew.

If that had happened today, the chicken would probably still be on the roof and Grandma would be stewing a plucked and dressed 69¢-a-pound hen from the supermarket.

Grandma Was a Sailmaker

~19~

FREE FOR THE TAKING

"Hey, Pete!" The voice tried to penetrate my thoughts.

"Pete!" Awareness slowly began to sink in. That was how a few folks pronounced our surname.

I was lying on my back, gazing at the fluffy, white clouds drifting lazily across the south Lafourche sky. The sun was warm, but not hot. I lay among broom straw in the uncultivated field which stretched from behind our back yard all the way to the 40 arpent line.

No accident had caused me to be there. No illness had suddenly come upon me and reduced me to a weak, fallen creature. I was there by choice.

It must have been a Saturday or a summer vacation from school was in progress. Else, I would've been indoors doing homework, in the yard feeding the chickens, or busy with some other of my daily chores.

I was ten and had several assigned chores. Instead, I was in the field and I was conscious of having a good time. There were very few boys my age living in our *cote*, or neighborhood. Play opportunities with others came seldom. Most of the time I was left to my own resources for amusement. Today I had chosen to explore the field.

At some point, enthralled by the interesting sky, I had flopped on my back. Content to watch the ever-changing cloud patterns, I became lost in time and oblivious to the remainder of the universe.

"Hey, Pete!" I was fully aware now of who and where I was. The voice still mystified me. I arose and looked around. No one!

"Pete, come see!"

Locating the direction of the voice, I recognized the caller as an older boy who lived four "fields" north of us. Now, understand that a field is no definite unit of measure. The term was used then to refer to the rear portion of someone's land, whether cultivated or not. Nor was a field usually any great distance in width, for the land already had been divided and re-divided many times. Always the division lines were at right angles to the bayou. Thereby, fields became narrower and narrower. Our field was 90 feet wide, others more or less.

"Pete, come see," the caller repeated.

Some five years my senior, he seemed to be occupied with some activity in his family's field. I made my way across the three intervening fields. As I approached, I became aware that he was picking ears of dried corn. Arriving, I dropped to a sitting position on the ground, ready to hear why he had summoned me.

"Do you want some corn to take home?" he asked?

"Doesn't your family want it?" I questioned.

"We have too much and Mama said I could give some away."

"If you're sure she doesn't want it," I said, "we

can feed some to our chickens. I'll go get a sack."

"No need for that. Here's an extra one. Take all the corn you want."

My opinion of this benefactor rose immediately. We had never had much contact. With the difference in our ages, we operated in separate boyhood circles. But here he was thinking of me when he had something to share! Wouldn't Mother and Dad be pleased when I brought home this thoughtful gift?

I broke off ear after ear after ear and dropped them in the sack. Soon the sack was bulging. Not quite full, you understand, for I had to leave enough free sack for a handgrip. I thanked my new friend more than once for his generosity. Twisting the free end of the sack in my hands, I strained every muscle to hoist the load to my shoulder. It moved but little and didn't leave the ground. I tried again. Same result.

I was faced with a dilemma! My choices were to leave some of the ears for a second trip, to take only what I could carry and not return, or to drag the loaded sack all the way home. I chose the latter. Not far across the fields on the way back, I was sure I had not made the most prudent choice. Carrying the corn was impossible for me and dragging it was not much easier.

Finally I reached our yard and dragged the sack to the back steps of the house. "Mama, Mama," I called.

Mother appeared at the door. Excitedly, I babbled the story. She understood enough to cause her to bound down the steps, grab my arm, and wallop the excitement out of me.

"You stole that corn!" she accused over and over again as she rained blow after blow upon my writhing body. Finally she stopped, more out of fatigue I suspect than compassion.

"I didn't, Mama." I protested. "He gave it to me."

"You will take that corn all the way back to their house," Mother directed sternly, "and you will give it to his mother— ONLY to his mother. Not to him, you understand?"

"Yes mam," I replied meekly. Tired but spurred on by the effects of the whipping, I dragged the sack back. This time I chose the roadside for a path. Gravel was easier to slide over than tall grass. I arrived. No one in sight!

Leaving the sack on the ground I knocked on the front door. The father was the one who came to the door. I asked to see his wife and soon she replaced him in the doorway.

I nervously explained, neglecting to mention the whipping I had taken. She uttered not a word to me, but walked to the end of the porch and called her son out of the back yard.

"Did you give away some of our corn?" she asked.

He stood awkwardly, barefooted, with the toes of one foot resting on the other. "Yes, mam," he answered hesitantly.

"Did I tell you to do so?

He shook his head. "No, mam."

You devil, I thought. You set me up!

"Why did you do it?" she persisted.

"I didn't feel like picking all that corn."

With no more time than it had taken my mother,

she too bounded down the steps. Grabbing him, she proceeded to administer to him the same fate which had befallen me earlier. The blows to his hide made me wince and the welts still smarting under my overalls hurt with every blow. But I felt no sympathy. Justice was being served!

Grandma Was a Sailmaker

~20~

RED EYE LEGACY

Cajun cuisine has earned world-wide acclaim. Master chefs from throughout south Louisiana are known for their culinary successes. Some have exposed the international public to the state's innovative and flavorful Cajun dishes. These achievements are to be admired. But I believe almost all Cajuns, men and women alike, can cook.

Few do not have personal recipes which they confidently can prepare as well as or better than anyone else. Most of these are tantalizing entrees. Though many recipes are titled similarly, there is found great variety in procedures and ingredients.

It has been said that a Cajun will eat anything which does not eat him first. But a friend residing in Lafayette (sometimes referred to as the Cajun capital) and the author of an immensely popular series of children's books as well as editor-in-chief of a cookbook, is credited with saying it better. She is reported to have said that Cajuns will eat anything which bites them first, thereby assuring that what they are about to eat is fresh and fit for the pot.

Like other Cajuns, I like to cook. I give my mother credit for getting me started early by assigning to me the task of scraping the skin off wet, tiny, fresh red potatoes. Grown locally, I don't know if these were

"Cajun" potatoes, or even if such existed, though I suspect anything grown or made by a Cajun could have claimed the status.

I detested the chore, especially carving out all those red eyes, and I don't know that I ever learned anything about cooking potatoes from it. But at least it got me into the kitchen. Later, I did learn to prepare Mother's chicken and sausage gumbo and some of other people's dishes before venturing into developing recipes on my own.

At the outset of our marriage, my wife and I reached an agreement that I would prepare and cook all wild game and seafood destined for our table. Being a non-Cajun, she is attuned to turning out respectable fare such as pot roast, potatoes, vegetables, and desserts (and decidedly squeamish about skinning, plucking, or peeling the covering off some creature from the wild).

That agreement has worked well into the second quarter-century of our marriage. Although she periodically issues the disclaimer that she's not much of a cook, our table has been graced by much delicious food from her culinary efforts and I have had the practice needed to develop and refine numerous recipes of my own.

Mother's chicken and sausage gumbo recipe was the simplest of its kind which I have encountered. I still use it to the delight of friends and relatives, although I have made slight modifications of my own (*) for reasons which I shall explain as you read along. I also added the word "Royale" to the title because partakers tell me it is indeed a royal treat.

Mother's Chicken and Sausage Gumbo Royale

1 large onion, chopped
1/2 cup bell pepper, chopped
1/4 cup celery, chopped
2 oz. salt pork, cubed small
2 lbs. smoked sausage, thinly sliced
2 small fryers or 1 large, cut into pieces
3 to 4 tablespoons gumbo filé
water as needed to fill pot (about 4 quarts)
salt, if needed
pepper, if needed
* 1/4 cup shortening, bacon drippings,
or olive oil
* 1/4 cup flour
* 1 large clove garlic, finely chopped
* 1 cup drinking wine
* 1 teaspoon Worcestershire sauce

This preferably is cooked in a cast-iron cauldron or Dutch oven. Make a roux of shortening, drippings, or olive oil and flour by stirring constantly to avoid burning. (Mother did not make a roux, but I like it for coloring and thickening). When rusty brown, add onions, bell pepper, and celery. Cook until onions are translucent.

Add salt pork and sufficient water to cover. Boil until pork cubes shrivel— about five minutes. Add garlic, sausage, and sufficient water to cover. (I like the flavor and reported health benefits of garlic; Mother used it in roasts, but was neutral where broths were concerned). Return to boil and cook ten minutes.

Grandma Was a Sailmaker

Add chicken pieces, wine, worcestershire sauce, and sufficient water to nearly fill the pot. (I use wine and worcestershire sauce for special flavor; Mother wasn't well acquainted with either of these for cooking. If you disapprove of alcohol, don't fret. The alcohol in the wine quickly evaporates and there remains only the flavor imparted by the grapes). Without allowing broth to run over, cook until chicken flesh can be separated from the bones.

If you wish to debone chicken, remove pieces with slotted spoon then debone and discard bones. (I do; Mother did not). Return chicken meat to pot. Taste broth and add salt, if needed.

If the gumbo is cooked a day before serving, the pot can be placed in refrigerator overnight. Fat will solidify on top and can be skimmed off before reheating, resulting in a healthier meal. Overnight "resting" also will allow flavors to permeate the broth more thoroughly.

Bring to boil. Sprinkle filé into hot broth and stir. Filé, finely ground sassafras leaves, imparts a peppery flavor so taste broth before adding pepper to taste. If you are troubled by possible unavailability of filé where you shop, do not despair. This can now be found in supermarkets and specialty shops almost nation-wide. Cook five minutes more and serve over rice in a soup bowl. Should serve six to eight, depending on size pot used.

It would have been fitting if I could have added red eye potatoes to Mother's best recipe. I'm sure I would have if she hadn't cooked gumbo.

~21~

MARDI GRAS MERRIMENT

"Throw me something, mister! Throw me something, mister!"

"Over here, mister! Please, mister!"

These cries have rung in the ears of everyone who ever has attended a Carnival parade in New Orleans— or watched one on television. The glitter of the floats and their riders, the splendor of the occasion, and the chance to catch souvenir throws— lots of souvenir throws— is sufficient to thrust adults and children alike into the world of make-believe.

Elaborate float parades are now held on several days during Carnival season in other cities and towns of south Louisiana, including Thibodaux, Lockport, and Golden Meadow in Lafourche Parish. But it wasn't that way at all when I was growing up. Mardi Gras Day (Fat Tuesday, the day prior to the beginning of Lent) was celebrated among the Wetlands Cajuns— but only that one day. There were no parades several days in advance. In fact, there were no parades with floats!

In Cote Blanche, where I lived, the parading was done by masked, costumed men who walked up and down the road incessantly throughout the afternoon. These were said to *courir le Mardi Gras* (run the Mardi

Gras), although none actually ran. The expression is the same as that which has received much publicity in recent years in connection with the unique Mardi Gras activities among the Prairie Cajuns of southwest Louisiana. There they dress similarly, but ride along country roads astride horses (a scarcer item among Wetlands Cajuns than pirogues) collecting ingredients for a community gumbo to be cooked at day's end. Whereas our area's walking *Mardi Gras* have given way completely to the use of floats, the Mardi Gras riders of the southwest persist— at least in some communities such as Mamou.

The parading of *les Mardi Gras*, as they were referred to in the plural, was viewed by adults and children standing by the roadside or sitting on the front porches of their Cajun houses. There was no "Throw me something, mister" to be heard, for souvenir throws were non-existent then. Instead, as the marchers passed, children and adults alike shouted "*Mardi Gras, chic à la paille*" (loose translation: Mardi Gras with hair of straw). The expression was likely derived from the common title, *Mardi Gras*, applied to all maskers and the equally common straw-like fake blond "hair" protruding from under every masker's headpiece.

The variety of their colorful, home-made costumes was duly noted by adult and child observers. Opinions as to which one was the "best *Mardi Gras*", meaning the best costumed, were freely given and sometimes heatedly argued.

At dusk the costumers wound up at Lee Brothers' Dance Hall for an evening of cruising the dance floor with the ladies. Whereas the Lee Brothers were otherwise very circumspect about the attire dancers were allowed to wear onto the dance floor, Mardi Gras was the exception. Dressing indecently or in poor taste would not have been permitted under any circumstance, not that anyone would have shown enough bravado to try it. But covered heads and outlandish costumes were acceptable and there was as much variety of dress in the dance hall as there would be if you collected one costumed rider from each float in every New Orleans parade during a single Mardi Gras season.

My activities on Mardi Gras Day were severely limited for two reasons. First, I developed asthma when I was five and had yearly spring attacks until I was seventeen. The alternating cold and warm humid weather of the season bode ill for my respiratory condition. Almost every Mardi Gras Day was spent looking at the jubilant parading men from a window in the seclusion of our front bedroom. Mardi Gras dances at Lee Brothers' usually were for others to see and do.

Second, my mother believed that masking and costume-wearing was a sin— a belief then as unerrodable as if etched in stone. And she bolstered it by periodic proclamations that she had inquired of our parish priest and he had confirmed her worst fears. So, when I was age five and my dear uncle bought for me a simple, but much desired mask, Mother stood her ground and ordered him to take it back.

It is somewhat comforting to know that in her later years, after Daddy opened a business in Houma and I was gone from the nest, Mother viewed the parades there, enjoyed them, and mellowed sufficiently to give up that idea of sin (or at least to forgive it). As for me, I have had no recurrence of asthma attacks— and once, just once, as an adult going to a Mardi Gras dance, I did costume myself as the Lone Ranger.

~22~

BOATS

I have a friend who, like me, grew up "down the bayou." He collects model boats. I don't, but I have had an interest in boats for as long as I can remember. It is strange that I did not become a boat captain or deckhand or, at least, the operator of a boat ways— a colloquialism for a timber frame-work on which a vessel is built or repaired and along which it slides in launching. In other geographical areas it is known as a type of drydock.

I suppose my interest in boats began when my dad carved a shrimp lugger for me out of driftwood found on Grand Isle beach. I recollect the enjoyment I had pulling my boat over the yard while dragging a tiny net to catch "shrimp" (leaves lying on the ground). The blacksmith shop and boat ways less than a hundred feet south of where we lived provided further stimulation.

My earliest experiences with the blacksmith shop were when the owner, Mark Pitre, fired up his forge, heated it to a red glow with hand-operated bellows, and melted a cupful of lead to pour into metal molds. The result was tin soldiers which he gave to those who had been watching. When older, I watched him heat, pound, and shape metal into utensils needed on farm and boat.

From home I could watch at an early age as

boats were pulled upon the ways by a huge one-cylinder engine bellowing a loud "put-put-put-put". The boats remained there for one or more days while their owners scraped old paint, made hull repairs, re-caulked between hull planks, then re-painted the hulls. To save additional drydock charges, the cabin and mast were always re-painted after the boat had left the ways.

When I was old enough, I ventured near the ways to sit for hours while studying the work. Red copper-painted bottoms contrasted sharply with white superstructures. I was struck by how massive the boats looked as they towered above me, only to regain normalcy when returned to water.

Later, I became skilled enough at lettering to earn spending money restoring names and identification numbers on re-painted boats, even at the rate of 10¢ a letter or number. When our country entered World War II in December 1941, the Coast Guard required all boats to have name and number painted on the cabin top as well as on both sides of the hull. This was for ease of identification from aircraft and caused my earnings to increase by one-third.

Most boats with which I was familiar in the Cut Off and Cote Blanche areas were named for people, predominantly females. There was "Little Sarah" owned by Harris Chabert, "Rosabelle" by Luderick Terrebonne, "Angelina" by Olivier Angelette, "Laurencia" by Paul Curole, "Parismina" by Percy Pitre, "Queen Of The Sea" by Hypolite Lefort, and "Princess" by Wallace Chabert. But there was also "Young Morrison" owned by Leo Pitre, "Sterling" by Wiltz Picou, "Robertson" (believed owned by a Pitre), and "Two Brothers" by Wilfred Lefort, all named after males. "P.L.E.G." owned by Pierre Gaspard was named for him and his three children— Leo, Lawrence, and Enosia. " C. & C." owned by Constant Callahan might have been named for a male and female or two of either kind.

Some boats were named for places. There was "Morgan City" owned by Victor Curole, "Broadway" by Jessie Curole, "New Broadway" by Syria Curole, "White Coast" by Paul Lefort, "Rhode Island" by my father Ignace Pitre, and "Equator" and "Olympia", owners unknown.

The "Clovelly" belonged to Joseph Authement and was named for Clovelly Farms, north of Cut Off. It was 55 feet long and had the appearance of a barge with pointed bow. Mr. Authement and his three sons, Jules, Warren, and Elmo, hauled firewood to the shrimp-drying platform at Manilla Village on the coast of Lafourche Parish. The boat could hold 20 cords 4' X 4' X 8'. The wood was obtained by navigating northwest along Bayou Lafourche to the Eymard Canal, thence to Bayou Blue, and southeast to the rear of the Authement property, where the cutting was done. When not thus engaged, the "Clovelly" transported sacks of onions and potatoes through the Harang Canal at Larose, across Lake Salvador, into Bayou Segnette, and to the New Orleans French Market on the Mississippi River.

"Early Rose" owned by Enest Pierce, "Lily" and "New Lily" by Antione Pitre, and "Flower of Louisiana" by Julien Pitre represented the flowers. "Sea Eagle" owned by Victor Pitre and "Nightingale" by Raymond Terrebonne were about birds. "White Water" belonging to Adam David, "The Winner" and "Sea Plane" to

Grandma Was a Sailmaker

Lufraid Pitre, and "Silver Moon" to Eumes Terrebonne were less identifiable by category.

Each boat name had its own uniqueness. For instance, I learned the sail boat of my sailmaking grandfather, Melfort Gaspard, was named "Maine". It came into being around the beginning of the 20th century and was named after the battleship "U. S. S. Maine"— sunk in the harbor at Havana, Cuba, February 15, 1898 and a cause of the Spanish-American War. The slogan "Remember the Maine" spread throughout the United States and Grandpa remembered when naming his vessel.

Of the many boats, I remember best the "P.L.E.G." which belonged to my uncle. It was powered for many years by a tall, one-cylinder Atlas engine which echoed its "put-put-put-put" against the landscape. The Atlas eventually gave way to a Ford Model B automobile engine. This had four cylinders. It was quieter and moved the boat faster.

In the years prior to the 1940's, boats were to most Wetlands Cajuns the primary means of transportation and livelihood. The lugger was a source of pride even when needing attention. With few exceptions, the owner "babied" his craft, giving its needs top priority over his own. It was this devotion which allowed my pleasant experiences with boats.

~23~

SATURDAY NIGHTS
AT LEE BROTHERS'

When I was in high school, Cote Blanche was not exactly the social capital of Lafourche Parish. Nor is it now. But teenagers of that day seemed to need or have time for much less entertainment than do their counterparts today.

Our settlement (you rightly couldn't call it more) had one movie theater and one dance hall, both owned and operated by the Lee brothers. The theater showed a western film (we called them cowboy movies then) once on Saturday night and a different film, usually a musical, once on Sunday night. The dance hall was open each Saturday night from eight to 12 with music furnished by an imported band.

With both theater and dance hall in operation, you can visualize that Saturday night was a big social extravaganza. Except for one thing. Both movie and dance started at eight. The movie usually lasted two hours while the dance continued for four. When your social life all week had been nil, who appreciated having to choose or to divide time?

With me the decision always was simple. Never did I have enough money on any Saturday night to first attend the movie and then the dance. It was always one or the other and, ever since I had become

87

of age to attend, the dance always won out.

My Saturday night routine was inflexible. I ate supper and bathe before seven. From seven to eight I listened on radio to The Hit Parade, a playing of the week's ten most popular songs. Meanwhile I dressed. My attire every Saturday night summer and winter was a freshly starched white linen suit. I had only two suits and the tan sharkskin one was reserved for Sunday morning church service, also throughout the year. Mother saw to that. But she also washed and re-starched my white linen suit each week.

As soon as The Hit Parade ended, I left the house and walked the half-mile or so to the dance hall, located on the bayouside across from the theater. In my pocket always was a dollar— and only a dollar. That was all I had to spend no matter what. Although less than some of my friends may have had, a dollar was a significant sum to me since I had been taught that it represented a full day's wages for a field hand.

Arrival at the dance hall resulted in immediate spending of the entire dollar I had. The dance was what was known as a "jitney dance", which meant a male dancer bought and used a nickel dance ticket for each song to which he wished to dance with a girl of his choice. Always I bought 20 tickets at once. And I was broke for the rest of the evening!

Dancing within a crowd can be and was hot, even in a building cooled by large exhaust fans at one end of the dance floor. A cold Coke or Pepsi or R. C. Cola could really take the edge off one's discomfort. But not for a fellow who habitually spent his entire dollar for dance tickets.

And dancing sure can and did develop an

appetite in a fellow, especially when the aroma of cooking hamburgers and onions wafted from the grill to the dance floor. One of Mrs. Clabert's mouth-watering fifteen-cent creations could really stem the tide of hunger. But not for a fellow whose only dollar already had been exchanged for dance tickets.

It took considerable skill to stretch 20 dance tickets over a near-four hour period. Leaving early or remaining till midnight while unable to dance was inconceivable. So a form of self-rationing always was in order and having the last ticket left for the last dance gave one a real sense of accomplishment. Sometimes, to assist with the rationing, I would walk into the adjoining bar area and watch others play the slot-machines. These "one arm bandits" held no particular magnetism for me and watching friends choose to drop their coins into the slots always reaffirmed my earlier decision to dance my full dollar's worth.

As the last strains of music ended, people left. A few traveled by cars— usually mothers who had escorted their daughters. The Lee Brothers bus, which had transported women folk (men were excluded) from Larose and Cut Off, began its return journey. A few like me walked home, but it always seemed they were going up-the-bayou instead of down, as I was. Striking off alone, I usually filled my pockets with clam shells from the roadside— ammunition to ward off the barking dogs which took exception to a late-night pedestrian intruding along the unlit roadway.

Thus were Saturday nights— all Saturday nights— at Lee Brothers' in the early 1940's.

Grandma Was a Sailmaker

~24~

IN HIS FATHER'S FOOTSTEPS

On a white background inscribed with black letters shadowed in red were the words which described my uncle as a trawl, tent, and tarpaulin maker and repairer. The cypress sign hung from a stout cross-arm nailed to a 4' X 4' wooden post firmly anchored into the ground next to his front gate. The sign was my handiwork, the product of a high school boy who loved this uncle, the finest man I have ever known.

My uncle, Pierre Gaspard, was kind, loving, trustworthy, and helpful. His word was his bond. The son from the first marriage of my widowed grandfather (the sailmaker), he worked hard both as a boy and a man and never had the opportunity for schooling. He lived his entire life neither able to read nor write, able to understand some English, but relying exclusively upon our native Cajun French for his words.

In the 1920's and 30's, Uncle trawled for shrimp in spring and fall and grappled for oysters in the winter. In summer he handmade or repaired trawls, tents, and tarpaulins for himself and others, a skill learned from Grandfather. I remember the long trawl usually suspended between mast and rear post while his boat was docked briefly during shrimping sea-

91

sons. In winter I saw the long-handled oyster tongs which lay neatly on the foredeck. In summer I saw him in a small workshop behind his home, the particular workpiece of that moment stretched across his lap.

The boat was sold in the early 1940's and Uncle turned fulltime to making and repairing. Thus was created the need for the sign I lettered. Sign lettering was a craft I had been engaged in for several years while reapplying names and numbers to freshly painted boats of the area at the rate of $.10 per number or letter.

Uncle's work from then until his retirement many years later produced hundreds of canvas tents to be hung over fishing boats, somewhat like an overhead awning, to protect workers from the hot sun blistering over the waters of the Gulf of Mexico. Likewise, hundreds more of tarpaulins to cover the ice, fish, and shrimp-laden holds of trawl boats or the beds of trucks which transported iced cargoes over land. The number of trawls made or repaired is unknown but great.

Many of the instruments which Uncle used in his craft were the very ones my grandpa and grandma (his step-mother) had sewn their sails with. The pommel (a large thimble fitting over the palm) and a hand sewing needle are now part of the permanent collection at the Center for Traditional Boat Building, Nicholls State University, Thibodaux, Louisiana. The eyelet maker (an iron rod tapered to a point on one end) which both Grandpa and Uncle employed is missing, but remains a vivid memory.

Uncle was known for turning out work of exceptional quality at exceptionally low prices. So much so that customers on many occasions tried to pay more than Uncle asked for. He always refused to accept what he felt was more than a fair price.

"Trawls, Tents, and Tarpaulins Made and Repaired" said the sign. What it didn't say anything about was the exceptional character of this man with great skilled hands.

Grandma Was a Sailmaker

~25~

SAVING THE CROP

Dawn peeked over the tall sugar cane stalks as six high school boys and the farmer reached his field. It was Saturday and another long workday loomed ahead, but there was neither sullenness nor complaining. Cane knives in hand, the five others and I awaited eagerly the farmer's signal to resume harvesting the cane crop.

Our country had been plunged suddenly into World War II when Japan bombed our military installation at Pearl Harbor, Hawaii, December 7, 1941. By fall 1942, with millions of men fighting the war and other men and women working in defense industries, farms were depleted of laborers.

Sugar was already a rationed item. South Louisiana's vital sugar cane crop faced spoilage in the fields unless a substitute means of harvesting could be found. There were no mechanical harvesters to do the job. These had not yet been invented.

The scrapbook is yellowed. Corners of some pages are folded. The covers bear small rips and tears. The pages are brittle, photographs faded. I do not remember who salvaged it or sent it to me during the late 1970's. But it tells its story as well today as it did in 1942, reporting how 30 Cut Off High School boys

Grandma Was a Sailmaker

(part of over 500 who saved the sugar cane crop parish-wide) hand-cut more than 320 tons of cane. From October to December, we worked the equivalent of two to two and a half days a week during schoolday afternoons, then returned for a full day on Saturdays.

Being teenagers, few of us had previously cut sugar cane except one stalk at a time for chewing. We divided ourselves into groups of three and were assigned to farmers on a need basis. Wielding the cane knife was an art to be mastered if we were to get the harvesting done and avoid serious injury.

Instructions and supervision were provided by each farmer. Especially dangerous was the upswing when the knife rose out of sight overhead and behind, bringing the hook close to head and neck. We also had to learn pacing. Cane was handcut by rows of three. The progression on rows one and two was kept even while the third or fly row cutter lagged a few yards behind. This allowed the fly row cutter to lay his cut cane in the valley between rows one and two, as had the cutters of those rows.

When loading the cane into mule-drawn wagons, the farmer thus had clear valleys between rows two and three and between three and the next number one row in which to walk the mules and roll the wheels of his wagon. Cane was weighed at a central bayou-side point, then loaded on barges for the trip to the mill at Valentine near Lockport.

A water jug and food sack were part of each worker's equipment. Cutting cane was tiring, thirst- and hunger-provoking. Water jugs were up-ended frequently. During the short mid-morning and mid-afternoon breaks, fruit or cookies stayed the appetite, but most workers looked forward to the half-hour noon break when each brought out his sandwiches. Under such conditions, a couple of fried bologna sandwiches could be mighty tasty even when consumed while sitting alongside cane stubble.

Most cane farmers whose crops were thus saved appreciated the service rendered to them and to the country. All boys assigned to a farmer worked as a team and were compensated at the standard rate regular harvesters would have received. For every ton of cane cut, the team was paid $1.00. Thus the 30 workers from our school earned in excess of $320.

By 1943, high school labor no longer was needed. German prisoners of war had been brought into the area parishes and, under guard, they harvested the crops of '43, '44, and '45. P.O.W.'s were kept in compounds at night. The Lafourche compound was located near the sugar refinery at Valentine. It consisted of wooden barracks surrounded by a woven wire enclosure topped with barbed wire. At each corner was a guard tower manned by soldiers of our army. The prisoners were well-fed and received excellent medical care. They seemed as happy to be away from the war raging in their homeland as had been the high school cane cutters when saving the crop of 1942.

Grandma Was a Sailmaker

~26~

IF I STEP ON YOUR FOOT...

"What will we do if one of us forgets his lines?" asked my friend and classmate.

"The other will have to take over," I replied.

"But how will we know exactly when to take over?" he continued. "If we both should talk at the same time, the judges will know we've made a mistake."

"Yes, they will," I agreed, "so each needs to be able to signal the other if he needs a takeover and then say some thing like 'I will now turn over the demonstration to my partner'.

"I have it!" I continued. "If I need you to take over, I'll step on your foot shortly before turning it over to you verbally. If you need a takeover, you do the same."

"Great!" my friend agreed. "We can use this for a needed takeover for any reason."

It was in early spring of 1943. My classmate and I had been selected to represent our high school in the boys senior demonstration team event at the annual 4-H Club Achievement Day. The demonstration selected by our club advisor was pig vaccination. The script had been carefully written to include detailed explanations of purpose, procedure, and application of medication.

Grandma Was a Sailmaker

We had been taught to attentively remove the young pig from the crate in which it would be contained so as not to allow its escape. An escaped pig would mean a terminated demonstration and a score of zero for our school in that event.

We had practiced actual vaccinating by catching and innoculating the entire crop of young pigs of a local farmer. We knew what we were about as a demonstration team and had high expectations of winning first place. It had been decided that my classmate would do the actual vaccinating while I was to retrieve the pig from the crate and hold it for the needlework. All that remained was mastery of the wording of the script. And that was what we were practicing on the day our takeover plan was developed.

Achievement Day arrived and so did we bright and early at the host school. We carefully unloaded the crated pig, set up our demonstration table with its clean white cloth draping, and set the serum, hypodermic needle, gauze pads, and alcohol in place. We awaited the judges. And while we waited, we went over the script again.

After viewing several other demonstrations, the judges arrived at our location. They set up their folding chairs and, scoresheets in hand, signaled for our demonstration to begin.

I was first to speak and I handled my lines flawlessly. Then I turned the demonstration over to my classmate, who did equally well. I could tell both of us had a good feeling about how effectively we were dispensing our information to the judges. My turn came again and things continued to go right. Finished with my speaking part, I returned control of the demonstration to my colleague for the final time. He skillfully began his description of the actual vaccination procedure we were to do.

It was now time for me to get the pig out of the crate. I unlatched the cage door and reached in. I winced with pain as the ungrateful patient-to-be clamped its teeth on the little finger of my left hand. Blood spewed everywhere, it seemed. Nevertheless, I grabbed the pig with both hands and hauled him to the tabletop.

Seemingly oblivious to what had occurred, my classmate continued his monologue while readying the needle. He did the innoculation while I firmly held the squirming pig. "He is really cool," I thought, "doesn't get flustered easily. The judges have seen my bleeding finger, I know, and so has he (by now I had bled on my hand, on the pig and on the white table covering as well). Hey, I'll bet we can make some extra points with those judges if I add first aid for a pig bite to our demonstration."

I listened carefully to what my colleague was saying. A few lines before he was to go into his summation of the demonstration, I stepped on his foot. He took no notice. I stepped on his foot again. Still no reaction. As he prepared to begin the summation, I STOMPED his foot. Undeterred, he went through the summation, thanked the judges, and ended the demonstration.

After the judges moved to another location and I had returned that biting hog to its crate, I questioned my partner. "Why didn't you turn the demonstration over to me when I stepped on your foot?"

"I didn't know you stepped on my foot," he replied.

"Didn't know?" I questioned further. "I didn't only step on your foot, I stomped on it! I wanted to give myself first aid for my pig bite and tell the judges what I was doing. I thought we might earn extra points for doing something so spontaneous."

"What pig bite?" he countered. "I didn't know the pig bit you."

"Where do you suppose all that red stuff on the table came from?" I asked as I poured alcohol over the wound and held several gauze pads tightly against it. And he looked about him then, as if seeing for the first time.

~27~

GRANDMA'S HOUSE

Grandma's house was not Grandma's house. I thought it was when I was growing up and have referred to it that way all my life. I probably always will. But Grandma's house was really Uncle Pierre's house and his children, Leo, Enosia, and Lawrence, were correct when they referred to it as "Papa's house".

The house was built for Grandpa Melfort Gaspard, his first wife Clothilde Curole, and their four children. They had survived the devastating Hurricane of 1893 at Cheniere Caminada on the Lafourche Parish shore. His wife contracted pneumonia during the storm and died soon after they moved into the house. When Grandfather married my grandmother, Marie Annelie Bruce, in 1901, the house and property remained solely his since it was not community property.

Grandpa died in 1906 and his property was divided among two surviving children from his first marriage and one from his second. Daughters Ursula and Julie were dead and left no heirs. Cecile, Pierre, and Blanche (my mother) each received one third, the portion with the house going to his only son, 13 at the time. The house continued to be Grandma's home while Pierre grew up and married. His wife, Aliza

Grandma Was a Sailmaker

Marie Martin, died of influenza at age 21, leaving children of three years, two years, and a few months. Grandma took over the mothering of Pierre's children and largely reared them to adulthood while their father was away shrimping and oystering.

Grandma's house was what today would be called a "Cajun Cottage". Over the front half was a high hip roof slanting to front and rear. On the peak was where the chicken was perched, as reported in the essay, "Chicken, Anyone?". Over the rear half was a lower hip roof, slanting side-to-side and connected into the higher roof. Behind this was a short step-down addition the width of the house, covered by a shed-type roof. All roofs were of split cypress shingles. Outside walls were covered with lapped cypress boards weathered to a silver grey. The bottom half of the glass windows were covered by frames of mosquito screening. These were built to Grandma's specifications by Leo, when he was in high school. All doors were double paneled and locked at night by means of two large *crochets* (hooks). None of the doors, closed at night, had screens.

One entered Grandma's house from the front by climbing three or four wooden steps to the porch, which stretched the width of the house. A *balustrade* (railing) once encircled the porch, but later was removed during floor repairs. On the porch there usually were rockers and, sometimes, a pan of Grandma's yeast cakes drying in the sun.

Centered in the front wall was a doorway leading into a modest sitting room with front window and fireplace on the side wall. Opposite the doorway was a hall which provided access to two bedrooms on the left and one on the right, behind the sitting room. One on the left accommodated Uncle and the other the boys, who slept together. The one on the right was for Uncle's daughter. The hall emptied into a huge kitchen-dining room. To the left was a bedroom nearly of equal size (Grandma's bedroom).

In the kitchen-dining room were a fireplace in the middle of the long inside wall, Grandma's black cast-iron woodstove in which she baked her tea cookies and sweet potatoes, a long dining table with bench against the wall for the children to sit on, and other items of furniture such as chairs, rockers, and a *garde-manger* (larder) with screened doors and two drawers. The stove later was replaced by a larger, more sophisticated cast-iron stove with white and blue oven door and an upright back with a two-door storage area for baked items. This stove was suitable for burning either wood or coal and was won by Enosia in a raffle conducted by Ernest Gaspard's General Mercantile Store.

A side door led outside to two wooden cisterns which held rainwater for drinking, cooking, and washing. A rear door provided access into the half of the step-down addition which served as Grandma's pantry. On the wall next to this doorway was her coffee grinder. On the other side of the doorway, a water bucket complete with dipper was set on a stand. This was the dipper with which Grandma dampened the bread slices before adding sugar to complete my afternoon snacks, as told in "Grandma's Bread Snack".

The only window had an outside shelf to accomodate a dishpan in which plates, pots, and flatware were cleaned after each meal. Inside, the pantry was lined with shelves filled with food items. A rear door in the pantry permitted access to a third wooden cistern. In times of drought, neighbors finding themselves with empty cisterns came over to "borrow" from this rare, three-cistern family.

As Grandma's arthritis continued to worsen and she could hardly get around, she prepared their food in the pantry. A small table and two-burner kerosene stove were her mainstays. She reached pantry items by swiveling herself on a non-swiveling chair and pulling them closer with her walking cane.

Grandma's bedroom contained a double bed with massive posts and canopy, surrounded by mosquito netting. Its size seemed to offer protection and it was near the bed that I hid to escape the squeals of my pet pig, related in the essay "A Boucherie to Remember". On the bed were three mattresses— one each of corn shucks, Spanish moss, and down. In warm weather, the corn shuck mattress was on top and the down mattress on the bottom. When the weather turned cold and warmth was needed, the two were reversed. The moss mattress remained in the middle to provide a degree of firmness.

In the room also were Grandma's foot-pedal sewing machine, an *armoire* (wardrobe), two trunks, a large dresser with four drawers and a big mirror, at least one rocker, and other furnishings. A side door led to the outside and a rear door into the half of the step-down addition which served as her bathroom. In the latter were the *lavabo* (lavatory)— consisting of the traditional ceramic pitcher and bowl on a stand, a small facial mirror affixed to a wall, the No. 3 galvanized tub which served as the bath tub, and that greatest nighttime necessity— an enameled chamber pot with cover. Grandma's arthritis later caused someone to cut a round hole in an ordinary wooden chair and fit the chamber pot underneath.

Grandma's house provided for me countless moments of excitement, enjoyment, security, and refuge. Grandma's was at once both an adventure and a safe haven— even if the house wasn't hers.

Grandma Was a Sailmaker

~28~

CUT OFF IS NOT COTE BLANCHE

"All Cut Off ticket holders off at this stop," said the Greyhound bus driver as he braked the big bus to a halt near the Cut Off pontoon bridge. One or two passengers arose and stepped out as the driver opened the door. I remained seated. We were still three or four miles from where I lived at Cote Blanche. This was my first trip home in a month and I could feel the excitement mounting.

In June 1943 this Cajun, fresh out of a high school graduating class of 11, had arrived on the Louisiana State University campus. It was only my third time there, the most recent having been the previous summer. Then, I had spent the better part of a week participating in the 4-H Club poultry judging contest. The earliest had been a school-sponsored trip to attend an LSU-Mississippi State football game, my first college game to see.

I suppose it was the 4-H trip which convinced me LSU was where I wanted to pursue a journalistic career. I certainly hadn't done very well deciphering the university catalog which I had requested except to determine that such a major was offered there.

My parents drove me to the campus, witnessed the haircutting administered then to all freshman men, and soon departed for home, probably feeling

109

uneasy at having a hairless son.

The events surrounding my arrival and my parents departure left me with a certain degree of qualmishness. I soon was filled with enthusiasm again, however, by the realization that I was embarking upon the greatest adventure of my young life. Fortified by the feel in my pocket of a checkbook representing a bank account totaling a full $180, I figured this, plus the $10 per semester legislative scholarship I had been promised, would adequately cover tuition, room and board, and books for the academic year.

At registration the following day, I watched much of my finances disappear. It could have been even worse. The legislator who had promised the scholarship had over-committed and there was none left for me when I registered. Fortunately, the very nice director of financial aid, Mr. T. K. McKnight, placed a telephone call to a north Louisiana legislator who still had scholarships and secured one for me.

I realized I would need some means of replenishing my finances in time for the next academic quarter. I had little work experience except janitoring, gardening, yard work, and painting names on shrimp boats. But I could write and I was here to major in journalism. I decided that would be my Ace card!

On a Saturday afternoon soon after, the LSU baseball team played in Alex Box Stadium on campus. I attended and noticed that no student press seemed to be covering the game. I took careful notes, wrote a story with accompanying box score, and slipped it under the office door of *The Reveille* student newspaper. It was published in the next issue and I was invited to become a sports reporter. When the sports editor was drafted at the end of the summer quarter, I was named to replace him. I then began to earn $3.20 an issue, the solution for my troubled finances.

After the first month of being away from home, the need to return for a visit was almost unbearable. I had no means to travel the eighty or so miles except by Greyhound bus. Freshmen had been made to schedule at least one Saturday morning class, I suppose to discourage frequent trips home. My visit would be short, but I was determined. As soon as I was out of class, I was on the campus-to-town bus line, suitcase in hand. And within thirty minutes I had purchased a Greyhound ticket and was aboard the bus headed for home.

The once-a-day trip beginning at Baton Rouge and ending at Golden Meadow was long and tedious, requiring over five hours and dozens upon dozens of stops. Passengers boarding or descending were accommodated by stops anywhere along the line and the bus frequently was crowded to the point of standing room only.

So, after crossing the Mississippi River bridge in north Baton Rouge, we crept through Port Allen, Plaquemine, White Castle, Donaldsonville, and nearly a dozen smaller communities with names as impressive as Cut Off and Cote Blanche. At the Thibodaux bus station we had a rest stop rendered not so restful by the realization that the station manager anxiously awaited our departure to close up for the night.

On board again, turtle-pacing through St. Charles, Raceland, Lockport, and Larose plus the miles between. Finally, the Cut Off bridge!

"All Cut Off ticket holders off at this stop."

I remained seated while the one or two Cut Off passengers left the bus. As it inched forward again, I sat on the edge of my seat anxiously taking in the familiar though dimly-lit scenes. There was Cut Off High School across the bayou... and Lee Brothers Dance Hall and theater...and Ernest Gaspard's General Mercantile Store...and...and...our house!

I pulled on the stop cord and the bus halted in front of our gate. Having gathered my suitcase in one hand, I handed my ticket to the driver with the other and turned to step off the bus.

"You don't have a Cote Blanche ticket!" he exclaimed in a loud voice. Everyone on the bus stared. "You have a Cut Off ticket!"

I started to apologize, but he cut me short. "You owe the bus company another nickle. Cut Off is not Cote Blanche!"

Reaching into my pocket, I was greatly relieved to locate my only nickle. I gave it to him and quickly stepped off the bus. I felt embarrassed. The error had been mine, but it had not been deliberate. After all, what teenager in his right mind willingly would endure the stares and smirks always generated on the faces of ticket agents and eavesdroppers when hearing the order of a ticket to "Cut Off?" A ticket to "Cote Blanche" evoked no such response and was well worth the extra nickle!

~29~

A BURDEN TO BEAR

I find that I have a tendency to read the obituaries more often these last few years. It is not an obsession, you understand. I never read a whole notice unless it is someone I have known well. I look at the names because I am intrigued by how often nicknames are included.

Some of the more unusual nicknames which have appeared recently in area newspapers are "T-Beb", "Pip", "Dee", "Brud", "Frog", "T-Nat", "Potsy", "Crip", "Ticker", "Bebe", "Fat", "Mutt", "Bozo", and "Tiger". There have been also "Skip", "Poochie", "KiKi", "Cutch", "Fatty", "Rabbit", "Smoke", "Boonie", "Ka Toot", "Boogie", "Tutty", "Coppee", "Pourri", and "Nin". Not to remain unmentioned are "T-Coon", "Man", "Colo", "Shorty", "Stump", "Mano", "Teal", "Sweet", "Tinker", "Pappy", "Ham", and "Sugar Babe".

Most people, I suppose, have had a nickname or two in their lifetime. I am no exception. I wonder, though, how many of these have disliked what others have called them. When a deceased person's nickname is included in the obituary notice, it makes me question whether the person would have consented to this final use of what could very well have been a heavy burden carried through many years.

Grandma Was a Sailmaker

I was christened Vernie Anthony Pitre by my parents. My given name was that of a character in a novel my mother read during her pregnancy. As a young child, I didn't give much thought to names. As I grew older, however, I realized that some people didn't use my given name. That didn't make me unhappy because I didn't like it anyway. Trouble was I usually didn't like what they called me either. Made me wish a person were known by some number until old enough to pick his or her own name.

My earliest recollection of a nickname was "T-Vern". This was used by my grandfather, aunts, uncles, and numerous other adults, but not Grandma. She used my given name. One adult with whom I was well acquainted from first grade through high school called me "T-Van". I never knew if he couldn't pronounce "Vern" or really believed I was named Van something or other.

Nicknames for others became apparent to me sometime after I started school. Friends or acquaintances carried such handles as "T-Noote", "Coco", "T-Lui", "Poppo", "Blue", "T-Neg", "Night", "Mo-mo", "Yanse", "Din", "T-Vin", and "Shine". It was at this time that many of my male peers decided individually (not likely) or collectively (most likely) on a nickname for me.

Daddy smoked cigars from my first recollection of him until he died of lung cancer in 1981. He smoked them, but he never chewed the unlit end. This he accomplished by holding each cigar mid-mouth with his lips, never shifting it to either corner of his mouth as most other cigarists do. The result was a projecting appendage which resembled the prow of a ship. My peers, of course, gave me the ignominious nickname of "Cigar" and it plagued me until I left the bayou to enter the university. I was the only one of my high school graduation class to seek higher education so the nickname fortunately died with my departure. The years since have not been as unkind, but the matter of what to call me remains unresolved. When my wife and I met she did not like "Vernie" so she called me "Vern". That suited me fine and I began to use it, too. But some other folks who heard "Vern" concluded it must be a shortened version of "Vernon" and that's what they began calling me.

I hit on the perfect solution, I thought. I added an "e" to "Vern". No one now would think that "Verne" was short for "Vernon" and the worst anyone could conclude was that I mis-spelled my own given name. My wife, however, doesn't like the extra "e". She continues to use the original spelling, "Vern", despite my requests to the contrary. And someone wrote to me the other day and spelled my name "Verné", giving it the same pronunciation as it originally had.

Oh, well, just call me 438-40-5127.

Grandma Was a Sailmaker

~30~

THE GOOD OLD DAYS

Someone has said that grandchildren are better to have than children because, when they tire you out, you can send them home. I don't know how much I agree with this, but I do know I like being a grandfather. There is something magnetic about the little tots— and the older ones, too— as they discover the excitement of the world we live in.

If our lifestyles were not changing so rapidly and more of the customs of early Cajun childhood had endured, I would now spend evenings in a comfortable rocker, my grandchildren gathered around my feet as I continued the tradition of Cajun story time— a favorite form of *faire la veillé*. There would be no TV or stereo blaring, no ringing telephone to steal the attention.

At the evening, while still savoring the gumbo and other delicacies of a just completed Cajun supper, my wife and I would await arrival of the grandchildren. The supper dishes would have been washed and put away, the animals fed. I would finger my worn pipe (no longer lit now because of discoveries about the causes of lung cancer).

First would arrive Ryan Kathleen, always eager for a story, accompanied by Jennifer, her stepsister.

Close behind would be Dana Marie, the outdoor girl nevertheless fond of stories. The group would be swollen by the arrival of Lucious, Bernadette and Denny, the younger ones. Lastly would enter Celeste, oldest of the grandchildren, wanting still to participate but now troubled by the thought she may be too old for such as this.

"Pa-paw, tell us a scary story," one would say.

"Tell a story about animals," another would suggest.

Others, yet too innocent to be credited with tongue-in-cheek remarks, would chorus, "Tell us a story about the good old days."

I would have lots of stories about the good old days and for tonight I would select a story I call:

Pierre and the Squirrel Tree

It is before dawn of a 1928 winter morning in the Barataria section of southeast Louisiana. The weather is clear and icy cold and frost covers everything. Moonlight is all about as a thin, muscular man carries large bundles of furs to the bayou bank. Young Pierre sits alone in the *pirogue* (elsewhere known as a Cajun canoe) and watches. The bundles, except for the small one already nestled at the boy's feet, are much too heavy for the ten-year-old to be of help to his father.

Winter is trapping season in the marshes and along the bayous of south Louisiana. Trapping is an austere, but somewhat adventurous life, not only for the trapper but for his wife and children, too.

Trappers like Pierre's father, Henri, are very busy these days. Furs have to be taken from marsh animals, stretched inside-out on wire molds, cleaned, and cured several days in the sun before being ready to sell.

Today, it is time to travel across bays and up the bayou to Voisin's Store. There, Father will sell the first batch of cured furs for enough to keep his family fed and clothed this winter.

Pierre is making the trip with him. A boy has to begin learning lessons of livelihood early and Pierre has helped father in the preparation of the furs. Accordingly, a small bundle has been designated as his. Today Pierre will learn about selling. But Father will be the one to bargain for top price for the boy's share.

Cold weather has come early. The pelts are rich with thick, soft fur and should bring a good price. There should be enough money for the usual beans, rice, sugar, flour, and other staple groceries, for needed non-food items, and a little left over to be saved. Perhaps there will be some for a thing or two which the family does not expect. Surprises are exciting, even for the hard-working Henri and his devout wife, Adele.

Father loads the big *pirogue*, careful to evenly distribute the weight of the furs. Pushing the *pirogue* from the bank, Henri steps in and sits on the rear seat. "Don't move, my son," he cautions. Soon Henri's rapid but graceful paddle strokes are sending the sleek *pirogue* swiftly through the water.

Cajuns say *pirogues* can travel on a heavy dew. This journey, however, is across bays and into a deep bayou navigated by large boats. To overturn into the icy water could mean loss of their lives as well as the

Grandma Was a Sailmaker

valuable cargo.

"Papa, I like to go places with you," says Pierre, "even when I must get up very early." Henri smiles at his son. He enjoys Pierre and takes him along whenever he can. Sometimes he wishes for a road on which to travel instead of having to paddle the *pirogue* almost everywhere he goes. But Henri and his family need to be near the trapping grounds. The nearest road ends at Voisin's Store, several miles north.

"It just is not practical," Henri tells himself, "to think of a road stretching across the wet, boggy marsh. Why, the clam shells would sink clear out of sight!"

Of the trappers who work these marshes, Henri is one who cannot yet afford a motor boat of his own. *Pirogue* trips, however, are beneficial— providing Henri and Pierre hours to spend together. They can talk and enjoy the quiet which travel by paddle makes possible.

The rapid strokes of the paddle warm Henri's blood and he cannot feel the bite of the chilled air except when it enters his lungs. Pierre is hunched low on the front seat, sheltered by the furs.

The moon seems brighter than ever. They clearly see both banks of the bayou. Pierre wonders who has traveled these waters since the Indians and early Cajuns. He remembers his grandfather's tales of pirates... Pierre's thoughts are interrupted suddenly as he notices something, alerted at their approach, slip quietly from the bank into the water.

"Papa, what is that?" he asks. Henri has seen the movement, too, and knows it is one of the furry animals which lives in the marsh.

"It's a muskrat or a mink," is his reply. Henri

adds that these are plentiful this year. That is one reason the trappers like himself expect to earn more money than they have for several seasons past.

Their attention is diverted from bank to sky as they hear a familiar "Honk! Honk!"; "Honk! Honk!".

The sound is repeated over and over again. Although unable at first to see the source, Father knows it is honking by a flight of geese. Soon he sees the familiar V-formation as the geese fly across the bright moon. He counts nearly 40 in the flight.

"There are the geese!" he exclaims to Pierre, pointing toward the moon with his upraised paddle.

Calls and flight formations of geese and ducks, which winter by the hundreds of thousands in Louisiana, are as familiar to Henri as the tri-cornered grass of the marsh. They serve as an important food source for trapper families and provide enjoyment with their colorful plumage and unforgettable chatter. Their down, of course, makes excellent stuffing for soft pillows.

"What a beautiful sight," Father remarks to Pierre as the honking becomes more and more distant. Pierre nods his agreement.

The sighting reminds Henri of Adele. She has strong feelings about such things. "The good Lord gave us ducks and geese and rabbits and squirrels," the family has heard her say many times. "But these are his treasure and we are not to waste it."

The sun has just risen when the pair arrives at Voisin's Store. It is a large, tin-roofed cypress building, unpainted and with few glass windows. Most windows are mere openings, covered by closed wooden shutters only when inclement weather rules.

Pulling the *pirogue* ashore, Henri unloads the furs. Then he carries the heavy bundles into the store while Pierre proudly shoulders his.

Alcide Voisin greets them warmly. "Good morning, Henri, my friend. Good morning, Pierre."

"Good morning, Alcide." Father replies and the two men clasp hands in friendship and greeting. Pierre smiles his greeting. Alcide leads the way to the warmth of the pot-bellied stove which keeps the winter chill out of his store.

"How about a cup of good coffee to warm you up?" asks Alcide.

"Can't think of anything better," answers Father. Alcide pours the thick black liquid from the enamel drip pot on the stove and hands the cup to Henri. Then he pours for himself. The friends drink as they talk.

It has been several weeks since they last met and there is much to share— so much, in fact, that the men have a second cup of coffee, then a third. One of the many things they talk about is Henri's new houseboat. Before this trapping season, the family spent winters in an old wooden and tar paper shack on the bank of a bayou near where Henri traps. After an unusually prosperous trapping season last winter, Henri had enough money to buy lumber and build the floating home during the summer. Now the family is better protected and more comfortable.

Tied to pilings driven next to the bank, the houseboat has been towed to the trapping grounds. Since Henri does not own a motor boat, he paid for the fuel and another of his friends, Guilbert, pulled the houseboat. After trapping is over, the houseboat will be returned far up the bayou and moored in front of the family's permanent home until time to trap again.

While Alcide and Henri talk, Pierre busies himself looking at goods in the store. There are sacks upon sacks of flour, beans, and rice. Loosely woven reed baskets air potatoes and onions. Large metal drums hold traps. Tables are laden with bolts of cotton cloth for making dresses, aprons, shirts, trousers, and undergarments. On the walls hang lanterns, lamps, and shotguns. Pierre looks closely at the guns. One, a single-shot .410 gauge with shiny walnut stock and deeply blued barrel, almost seems to call to him.

Coffee-drinking over, it is time for Henri and Alcide to tend to business. Seeing Father untie the bundles, Pierre makes his way to the men. He must learn how to sell furs. Father spreads the pelts on a long cypress table. Alcide picks up each pelt individually and examines it carefully. He places each in one of four piles, grading the pelts according to quality.

One pile, known as "tops", contains pelts of highest quality. They will bring the most money. Another pile contains pelts of middle quality, the third those of poorest quality. In the fourth group are "kits", the small pelts of young animals. These have a softer, smoother feel.

When grading is over, Henri and Alcide discuss the price to be paid for pelts of each grade. Pierre listens carefully. Alcide makes a first offer for the best pile, knowing that it will be less than Henri will accept. That is part of bargaining. "I'll give you sixty cents for each pelt," he says.

Father thinks only a little while, then counters

with, "One dollar and a half each."

The storekeeper raises his offer a little. "Seventy."

Henri lowers his asking price a little. "One dollar twenty-five."

After each has taken several turns trying to get the price most acceptable to him, the men agree on one dollar per pelt. The deal is sealed with a handshake. Then the process is repeated for each of the other groups of pelts.

Finally, Henri's pelts have been sold. Pierre's bundle is untied and bargained for. Pierre watches with close attention and grins broadly as he hears the amount his furs have brought.

It is time to buy provisions for the family and start the long trip home. "Papa, can I buy that .410 gun with my fur money?" questions Pierre.

"I'm afraid even with the good price Mr. Voisin is paying for your furs, son, you wouldn't have enough," answers Henri.

Pierre is disappointed, but determined not to show it. He has seen a litter of puppies through one of the store's windows. Pierre decides to go outside and pet the puppies.

Father buys large quantities of beans, rice, coffee, and sugar. A sack of flour is next, followed by other items the family will need during the next several weeks of the cold marsh winter. Among these are shotgun shells for himself. It is especially important that he remember shells because the family depends entirely on Father's hunting for their meat. Some they use fresh; the remainder either is preserved with salt, smoked, or cooked and stored in lard in large crock jars.

Alcide reminds him that Adele ordered material for clothing when they stopped at the store on their way to the trapping grounds the last week of October. It has arrived and Father feels sure its looks will please Mother. He buys thread and an extra supply of needles, too.

While the storekeeper is cutting and wrapping the cloth, Henri gazes at the shotgun Pierre has admired. He knows how much Pierre wants a gun of his own and remembers his very first. The boy has been hunting with Father many times. And Pierre has often asked when he can have a gun, promising to properly care for it and use it safely.

Each time Father's reply has been, "Pierre, one day I'll let you get one. But first you have to grow a little stronger and get a better notion of right and wrong in your head." This has endured since Pierre was six and Father carried the boy on his shoulders when they went searching for a good place to hunt squirrels.

The shotgun glistens at Henri from the wall. He begins to think this may be the right time and the right gun for Pierre. Alcide sees Father eyeing the gun. "Just got it in yesterday, Henri," he says. " I'll make you a good price . Pierre can have it for not much more than the worth of his furs."

"I know how much Pierre wants his own gun," Father thinks. So he buys it. There might have to be a little less beans and rice and coffee and sugar for the family later. But now Pierre can bring home his own shotgun and shells for it, too. Henri loves all his children and he does not forget to buy gifts also for

Marie Adele and Jacque, Pierre's younger sister and brother.

Pierre has tired of playing with the puppies and re- enters the store. He hears none of the talk between the two men. As he returns to where they stand, he sees Mr. Voisin take down the gun he has been hoping for. His heart sinks! Someone has bought it ! A tear trickles out of one eye. Quickly he wipes it away with his sleeve.

Imagine Pierre 's surprise as Father takes the gun from Mr. Voisin and hands it to him. "It is yours, Pierre," Henri says. "You have bought it with your furs. Use it carefully always."

As Cajuns say, Pierre is "beside himself", meaning he is overjoyed. He throws his arms around Father's waist and hugs man and gun tightly . "Thank you! Thank you!," he exclaims. " I'll be careful! I'll be careful!"

All the way home Father enjoys Pierre's excitement . With each stroke of the paddle he seems to hear again his son's gleeful thanks.

As the *pirogue* reaches shore next to the houseboat, Pierre excitedly jumps out. Marie Adele, Jacque, and Mother are all waiting for them. "Papa! Papa! Let's go shoot my gun!" exclaims Pierre almost before he shows the others his prize.

"All right," agrees Father, "but first let's unload the *pirogue*. Mother may need some of the things we've brought and Marie Adele and Jacque are wondering if they will be as lucky as you."

Everyone helps to unload. The younger children are delighted with the presents Father has picked out for them. Mother is proud of her new material and appreciates Henri's thoughtfulness in selecting matching thread and buying new needles.

"Let's go over there," Father points after the excitement has quieted. Pierre and Henri go a safe distance from the houseboat. Although Pierre had fired Father's 12 gauge shotgun as early as two years before, Henri had to help him hold the big gun. Now, Pierre is strong enough not to need help with his. Father shows him again how to load, cock, and shoot. Then, with Henri watching, Pierre proves he can do it alone.

Pierre is all excited about going to hunt for squirrels and wants to leave at once. Father says, "Now calm down, Pierre. You hunt squirrels best in the morning when they're out looking for acorns to eat. Besides, there's plenty time to try your new gun on game in the days ahead."

But Pierre is so excited and wants to go hunting so much that Henri finally agrees he can go the next morning provided, of course, he minds everything he has been taught about hunting carefully.

Sleep is not something Pierre can do much of this night. When he sees the first light of day, he dresses quickly and leaves with his new gun, forgetting all about breakfast.

Pierre walks very fast along the bayou bank, being careful to avoid boggy places. Otherwise, he could lose his footing. The Louisiana marsh in many places is a floating marsh. Pierre has been taught that carelessness could result in quickly being over his head in mud and water.

Pierre's haste scares a pair of French ducks, known elsewhere as mallards, from their early feeding place in a nearby pond. He is startled as they burst suddenly into the air. Seeing what has frightened him, Pierre pauses and admires their beauty as they hurriedly fly away.

A mile from the houseboat he turns from the bayou and comes eventually to a *chêniere*, one of several oak tree-covered ridges rising like islands in the marsh. Pierre moves very quietly among the trees. Father has taught him well.

Shortly he sees a fine squirrel tree. It is a huge live oak with big branches and many leaves. Live oaks do not lose their leaves in winter and provide excellent concealment for the furry little animals. Pierre examines the tree carefully, but sees no signs of squirrels.

From the acorns on the ground, Pierre knows squirrels come here for food when hungry or seeking to store winter supplies. Hungry himself from no breakfast and the long walk, Pierre finds a nearby log to sit on. Then begins the wait that all squirrel hunters know. Squirrels do not show themselves unless there has been no movement in the woods for a long while.

As he waits, Pierre's eyes search the big tree. Long strands of Spanish moss hang from its branches. The moss reminds Pierre of a story he has heard old people tell. The moss is said to represent the long hair of Evangeline, made famous in Henry Wadsworth Longfellow's poem about this most famous of Cajuns.

Evangeline and Gabriel, the man she was to marry, were forced from Nova Scotia aboard different ships. After seeking him for years, she died in Louisiana very sad and lonely. The trees then grew moss in her memory. Father has said that, although Evangeline never really lived, Longfellow modeled the character in his poem after a real Acadian named Emmeline LaBiche. He has explained further that Spanish moss thrives on air, using the tree only as a resting place.

Pierre spies movement out of the corner of his eye. Branches in a nearby tree sway as something scampers quickly through them. It must be a squirrel! Pierre is right. A big brown squirrel makes his way from tree to tree until he is on a branch in the tree near which Pierre waits. The squirrel looks at the bountiful acorns on the ground.

Pierre is excited, but careful not to make noise. He slowly raises his new gun, sighting the squirrel over the bead at the end of the barrel. Pierre is ready to shoot when the squirrel suddenly jumps to another branch and runs down the other side of the oak.

The squirrel is nowhere to be seen, but Pierre keeps quiet. Father has shown him how easily squirrels can be frightened. Soon the squirrel reappears. It runs up the tree again and stops.

Pierre raises his gun slowly and once more lines up the squirrel over the bead. He is mindful to remember Father's teaching about pulling rather than squeezing a shotgun trigger. This time Pierre shoots, but is distracted by a flash as he fires.

The pellets strike the branch next to the squirrel. The shot does nothin except scare away the squirrel and cause it to drop what has distracted Pierre. Whatever it is shines as it falls and disappears into the grass near the tree.

The boy rises quickly, forgetting the squirrel to search in the grass. He looks and looks until finally he catches a glint of something shiny. Pierre picks up an object round like a nickel, but much larger. Never has he seen anything quite like this before. Pierre forgets about hunting squirrels and hurries back to the houseboat as fast as his young legs can carry him.

"Papa! Mama! Look! Look!" shouts Pierre as he races up the walkway to the houseboat.

"Slow down Pierre," says Father. "You're all out of breath."

"Papa! Papa!" continues the excited Pierre, "I shot at a squirrel and look what he dropped when I missed him."

Henri takes the round shiny object and examines it carefully. Adele stares at it, too. Marie Adele and Jacque are almost as excited as Pierre in their anxiety to know what it is.

After a few moments, which to hungry Pierre seem longer than from one meal to the next, Father says, "This is an old doubloon— one like Jean Lafitte and his pirates are said to have buried around here long ago. Once, I saw one that an old oysterman brought to Voisin's Store. Pierre, show me where you found this."

Pierre leads Father to the squirrel tree. They search and search, but find no other doubloons. "We don't know where that squirrel first picked up this doubloon nor how far it's been carried," says Father. "Let's go home. We're not going to find that pirate treasure."

Great disappointment is all over Pierre's face as they return to the houseboat. He has neither the pirate treasure nor a squirrel to show off his hunting skill. His mother sees Pierre isn't feeling so fine.

"Pierre, my dear," she says, "You didn't lose a

treasure. You gained one. The good Lord made that squirrel give you something to keep which always will remind you of today."

Father adds, "You will never forget your first hunt with your own gun. Years from now you proudly will tell your children and grandchildren about it."

Pierre's face brightens. He turns the doubloon over and over in his fingers. His disappointment slowly melts into a wide grin.

Grandchildren are a treasure, too. They can make *raconteurs* (storytellers) of their grandparents by the mere suggestion of willingness to hear about the good old days. Each story session could continue far into the night were it not for our own children awaiting the return of their progeny for the realities of homework, baths, and compulsory bedtimes.

AFTERWORD

ABOUT THE AUTHOR

The author was born at 7 p.m., March 10, 1926, to Ignace Joseph Pitre, son of Maximillien Eveque Pitre and Leocadie Adelaide Dantin, and to Blanche Bernadette Gaspard, daughter of Melfort Francois Gaspard and Marie Annelie Bruce, wedded at Sacred Heart Catholic Church, Cote Blanche, June 15, 1925. The ancestral lines of seven great-grandparents are traced to Acadie (now Nova Scotia), the other to Italy.

It is interesting that the name Pitre is not of French origin although one of the original family names of Acadie. It is derived from Peters, one of a group of Scottish settlers who inhabited part of Acadie while the French, English, and Scots were contesting the area. When the Scots were recalled by their government, Peters remained with the French and the name gradually evolved into Pitre.

The surname of the author's maternal grand-mother was Bruce, but is traced to Genoa, Italy, where it was Brouze. The change in spelling is known to have appeared first in a neighboring Louisiana parish during the recording of a baptism in which her grand-father served as *parrain* or godfather.

After having been graduated from Cut Off High School in 1943, the author enrolled in Louisiana State

133

University until volunteering for the Army Air Force at age 18. He served in the south Pacific as radio operator aboard a B-29 bomber and participated in numerous raids over Japan. He was discharged with the rank of staff sergeant in 1946, having been awarded the Air Medal three times and other campaign decorations as well.

In 1947 he married Yvonne Marie Benoit of Houma, daughter of Lucious Joseph Benoit and Lillian Marie Crochet. To them were born a son, Dennis Michael, and a daughter, Darlene Marie. After nearly 15 years, the marriage was dissolved in 1962.

In 1950 he returned to Louisiana State University, joined the Air Force R.O.T.C., and was awarded the Bachelor's degree in education and a second lieutenant's commission in 1953. He retired from the Air Force Reserve in 1964, having attained the rank of Captain.

He has written creative stories and news and feature articles for newspapers, the earliest having been published during his high school years. Before settling on a career in education, he ventured into journalism. He worked in Houma, Louisiana, as news and sports editor for The Houma Courier. This was followed by a brief venture as part-owner of The Bayou News, an ill-fated weekly newspaper. He concluded with being news editor and French news broadcaster for Houma radio station KCIL-AM.

He taught in Terrebonne Parish schools from 1953-56, leaving to become assistant director of housing at LSU while completing the Master's Degree in administration and supervision. He joined the faculty of Nicholls State University in Thibodaux in 1957.

In 1963 he married Ouida Lorraine Boyette of Goodman, Mississippi, daughter of Edgar James Boyette and Hattie Melinda Burrell, and adopted Jacqueline, her daughter from a previous marriage.

For four years he worked intermittently on the Doctor of Education degree which was conferred by LSU in 1967. Having been named director of guidance services at Nicholls in 1960, he served in that capacity until becoming dean of student services in 1969. Meanwhile, during the Cuban Crisis of 1962-63, he also was dean of the college of education while the permanent dean was in the navy.

He had been instrumental in beginning the graduate school in 1965 and became its second dean in 1971. After 13 years as graduate dean and 27 years at Nicholls, he retired in August, 1984— timing that to coincide with Ouida's retirement as associate professor of student development and counselor.

Three weeks after retirement, the couple began an extended tour of the New England states. They have traveled since to most of the southeastern, mid-east, and mid-western states, but spend much time pursuing joint or individual hobbies such as playing Bridge, reading, writing, genealogy, crafts, painting, and landscape gardening.